Right Steps
For Kids

Pam Eddings

180-DAY KID'S DEVOTIONAL

FIVE LESSONS PER WEEK
FOR AN ENTIRE SCHOOL YEAR
ESPECIALLY FOR MIDDLE SCHOOL STUDENTS
OR FOR NEW CHRISTIANS

BY PAM EDDINGS

RIGHT STEPS FOR KIDS
180-day Kid's Devotional

By: Pam Eddings

ISBN-13: 978-1518798696
ISBN-10: 1518798691

Copyright ©2015 by Pam Eddings

All scripture quotations in this book are from the Authorized King James Version of the Bible unless otherwise noted.

ALL RIGHTS RESERVED. No part of this publication may be reproduced or transmitted in any form or by any means, electronic or mechanical, including photocopying, recording, or by any information storage and retrieval system without prior permission of the author, with the exception of short quotes that are properly credited.

Edited by Jaime Maddix
Cover Design by Ken Raggio
Image: Boy Walking Toward Light, ©Haywiremedia, Dreamstime.com

For information, to schedule speaking events, or to order books by Pam Eddings, please communicate by email with **eddingspam@gmail.com**

FOLLOW ME on TWITTER: pameddings
FRIEND ME on FACEBOOK: Pam Eddings

Table of Contents

Dedication 7
Foreword 9
Introduction 11
God's Word Is True 13
Know God's Word 18
Love God's Word 23
Marriage – God's Way 28
Correction Develops Character 34
Wise Words From King Solomon 39
Old Testament Heroes 44
Ten Commandments 51
More Old Testament Heroes 58
David – God's Boy 65
Families Working For God 71
Jesus Loves Children 77
New Testament Heroes 82
There Is Only One God 89
You Must Be Born Again 95
Basics For New Believers 101
Love Covers All 107
Prayer 112
I Love My Church 117
Wise Words From The Apostle Paul 122
The Joy Of Giving 128
Fruit Of The Spirit (Part 1) 133
Fruit Of The Spirit (Part 2) 138

Growing Fruits Of Righteousness (Part 1)	143
Growing Fruits Of Righteousness (Part 2)	149
Be A Hard Worker	155
Be A Godly Example	160
God's Holy Children	165
7 Sins God Hates	170
Things To Throw Away	175
More Things To Toss	180
My Body – God's Temple	186
Miracles For Children	191
Modern Day Heroes	198
If You Will, God Will	205
Wrapping It All Up	211
Answers to Weekly Reviews	217
Index	223
About the Author	231

Dedication

To my five beautiful grandchildren:
Kevin, Ryder, Molly, Bethany, and Kristen.
This book of children's devotions has been written
as a labor of love from your Grandma Pam,
who was asked to add to your Bible training at home
by writing some of my devotional thoughts
which have been gleaned from 60+ years of
being a student of the Bible.

To my sons, Russell, Raymond, and Rodney
and my daughters-in-law, Ashley, Desiree, and Jazmin.
I prayerfully pass these devotional writings to you
to read and discuss with your children.

To grandparents, parents, children,
and brand new students of the Bible.
May you also prayerfully read
and study the contents of this book
as you ascend these Biblical steps - "Right Steps"
on your journey to your eternal, heavenly home.

Foreword

During the summer of 2015, our family made the decision to remove our oldest son Kevin from public school. There are several reasons why we made the decision to homeschool. In time it will prove to be a great blessing for all of us. I knew that I wanted to begin our day with Jesus and Bible reading, so as I began to pull scriptures that I wanted Kevin to learn, I thought it would be wonderful if he had a reference book to help him through the emotional challenges of growing up. So many times as parents, we tell our children that "Jesus does not like it when you behave in a certain way." The problem is that telling children is not the same as having them learn things for themselves.

I wanted my children to learn to process their emotions from the inside out, so I asked my mother-in-law to write a book that did just this. She accepted the task, and now when my children are angry, scared, unforgiving, selfish or hateful, I can refer them to their devotional books for an explanation of the emotion in question and its scripture location in the Bible, so they can reflect on their actions in a positive and non-confrontational way. I am a firm believer in self-taught greatness. Learning is much more effective when we can see, touch, hear and speak the topic at hand. I am so thankful that Pam chose to take on this project.

Right Steps For Kids will help our family train up our children, and teach them to seek Jesus for guidance and support. Thank you Pam for all that you do!

Ashley Eddings
Marionville, MO

As a grandmother to my two daughters, Pam has been a wonderful influence in their lives. Pam is a consistent Godly lady who shows them how to live the principles in the Bible. She is often reading or teaching Bible stories to Bethany and Kristen. As a homeschooling family, Bible devotions are an important part of each day. For our devotions with the girls, we love to read Pam's *Bible Gems* book. Instilling the Word of God in their lives is very important, and we enjoy doing this through Bible Quizzing and daily devotions. I know both of my girls will enjoy reading and following along in Pam's new devotional, *Right Steps for Kids!*

Desiree Eddings
Springfield, MO

In a day when our children are inundated with so many words from so many sources, it's refreshing to have a source of life-giving words to share on a consistent basis with our kids. My sister, Pam, has always had a passion for God's Word, which is evidenced by her first two books, *One-Year Bible Quiz* and *Bible Gems to Start Your Day*. This book, *Right Steps For Kids* was written for her grandchildren, and it will also be a great blessing to your children and grandchildren!

Paula Murphy
Baton Rouge, LA

Our daughter, Pam, began her Christian journey at age nine and has devoted her life to being a student of the Bible. She has edited books for numerous authors over the years, but she has just recently assumed the role of author with the publication of her first two books, *One-Year Bible Quiz* and *Bible Gems To Start Your Day*. These two books have been a part of our daily devotions since each one was published. Her books reveal her deep love of God's Word and her desire for her readers to dig deeper into its pages to discover more of its truths. After reviewing *Right Steps For Kids,* we are certain that it will be a great source of information for children to learn Bible principles for daily living. We intend to use it in our daily devotions as well. Thank you Pam, for accepting the call to challenge children to develop a deeper understanding of God's Word.

Hubert & Gloria Nixon
Baton Rouge, LA

The habits of life begin early. Shower, brush your teeth, clean your room, and do your homework are all habits of a lifetime. The book you hold, *Right Steps For Kids*, is a tool to establish these habits! Thank you, Pam Eddings for this resource!

Rev. Carlton Coon
Pastor, Calvary United Pentecostal Church
Springfield, MO

Right Steps For Kids is uniquely designed with 180 lessons, and geared for a Monday – Friday structure that would be a perfect way to start your children each morning on a path to growing in God! Whether you are homeschooling your children or simply want to imprint Biblical principles on their hearts, this book is an excellent guide to help lead the way.

Jaime Maddix
Safety Harbor, FL

Introduction

When my daughter-in-law asked me to write a devotional book for my oldest grandson to use as a daily Bible study resource for his homeschooling, the subject was discussed among my family members, and before long, everyone got involved in this project. Ideas for topics and content were given by my sons and their wives, and I invited my five grandchildren to draw and color pictures that would represent the topics chosen for the book. Although four of them are younger than the target age for the book, I have included their signed artwork for a family keepsake. Kevin and I have discussed many of these devotions as they were being written so I could be certain that the material was understandable for the targeted age group.

I originally intended to write devotions mostly about good and bad behaviors, but as I continued to pray and search the Word, the nature of the topics I wrote changed to encompass so much more than that. Life isn't only about getting rid of bad behavior so you can be well-behaved. Because we are born into sin, a list of rules and regulations will not change our sinful nature. That change only happens when you experience the New Birth. Consequently, my focus for this book has changed from simply addressing inappropriate behaviors into developing a simplified guide for living the Christian life. While my target audience is middle school children, this guide could also be used by new believers who are just learning to study the Bible as well as parents and grandparents with their younger children.

Lessons on young heroes of the faith, families who served God together, the New Birth process, peer pressure, Christian virtues and inappropriate behaviors are just a small sampling of what you will find in this book.

Because a typical school year consists of 180 days, this book includes one devotion for each day of the school year. It is laid out in a weekly format with a different topic being discussed each week. Because I wrote with homeschoolers in mind, each week concludes with a Review page containing a quiz or other activity along with some memory work.

Obviously, Christian living principles can't be adequately taught in 180 lessons, so I have included numerous footnotes with scriptures and comments for additional study. As always, my goal for writing is to create a hunger to study God's Word and dig deeper into its pages. The hours of prayer, research and writing that have been invested in this project will be more than compensated if I can recruit more people to become lifelong students of the Bible.

Pam Eddings
October 2015

How sweet are thy words unto my taste! yea, sweeter than honey to my mouth!
Psalms 119:103

Week 1

God's Word Is True

 Day #1   God's Word Is Always Right

*For the word of the LORD is right;
and all his works are done in truth.*
Psalms 33:4

King Nebuchadnezzar learned the hard way that God's Word is true, and all His works are done in truth. The king told the prophet Daniel about a dream he had, and Daniel warned him that it meant he had better let God be the ruler of his life. But the king ignored the warning. One day he was walking around his palace, and he began bragging about building the great city of Babylon by his own power. Because he did not give any glory to God, he was driven from his kingdom into the field. He lost his mind and for seven years, he lived outside and ate grass like an animal. At the end of that time, God restored his mind and his kingdom. Most importantly, Nebuchadnezzar never forgot that the works of the King of heaven are true, and the King is able to bring down anyone who is too proud to give Him the praise and honor that He deserves.[1]

Prayer: *Lord Jesus, I surrender my will to you. If I start acting proudly because of my accomplishments, let me remember the story of Nebuchadnezzar, and change my behavior to show respect and honor toward you and your Word. Amen.*

 Day #2   God's Word Endures Forever

*Thy word is true from the beginning:
and every one of thy righteous judgments endureth for ever.*
Psalms 119:160

The Apostle John wrote that in the very beginning of time, the Word existed, and the Word is God.[2] Because God's very nature is true, everything He says in His Word is also true. Jesus taught that the world and the heavens would one day pass away, but His Words will never pass away.[3] That is a wonderful promise.

---

[1] Daniel 4:1-37.
[2] John 1:1.
[3] Matthew 24:35; Mark 13:31; Luke 21:33.

Prayer: *Lord Jesus, I believe that your Word is true from the first page all the way to the last page, and every one of your laws will endure forever. Help me to know your Word and live by its teachings every day of my life. Amen.*

 Day #3   **Treasure The Truth**

Buy the truth, and sell it not;
also wisdom, and instruction, and understanding.
Proverbs 23:23

The Psalmist writes in chapter 119 that God's law is Truth, and all of His commandments are Truth.[4] Every single word in the Bible is true, and those words will teach you how to get to Heaven if you will learn and obey them.

How much is Truth worth to you? Would you cheat on a test so you can get a good grade, rather than following the Bible's teaching to be honest? Would you rather tell a lie to stay out of trouble than to follow the Bible's teachings to tell the truth? The wise King Solomon advised you to buy the Truth and don't let anything steal it away from you. Obedience to the Bible is your ticket to Heaven.

Prayer: *Lord Jesus, your Word is very precious to me. If I make a wrong choice and disobey something in your Word, forgive me and help me to try harder next time. Amen.*

 Day #4   **God's Word Is True**

Sanctify them through thy truth: thy word is truth.
John 17:17

God's Word teaches you what sin is. Once you know what sin is, obedience to the Word - to the Gospel - will provide a way for your sins to be washed away. You will then act differently than sinners. Your obedience to the Truth of God's Word will set you apart as one of God's holy people.

---

[4] Psalms 119:142, 151.

Prayer: *Lord Jesus, as I learn more about your Word and live according to its teachings, let my life be a bright light to others who do not know you. Amen.*

Day #5   God's Word Is Inspired

All scripture is given by inspiration of God, and is profitable for doctrine, for reproof, for correction, for instruction in righteousness: That the man of God may be perfect, thoroughly furnished unto all good works.
2 Timothy 3:16-17

Every single word in your Bible was written by men who were inspired by God to write. The words were actually "God-breathed." Those holy words are useful to you in four different ways:

1. In those words you learn doctrines, which are the essential teachings and values by which you live your life.

2. Scripture teaches you what sin is, and when you do something wrong, the scripture reproves or scolds you for your wrongdoing.

3. Not only does the scripture scold you for your wrong; it also corrects you by telling you how to change your behavior.

4. Finally, the fourth purpose of scripture is to teach you how to live a righteous life.

When you allow the Bible to teach you in these four areas, you will develop into a mature child of God who is prepared to do good works.

Prayer: *Lord Jesus, develop in me a love for your Word, and as I learn it and live it, help me grow up to be a person who is an example of a true Christian in everything I say and do.*

 Week 1 Review

Answer True or False for each statement below.

____ 1. All of God's works are done in truth.

____ 2. God's Word can be used to learn doctrine, but not correction.

____ 3. God's Word has been true from the beginning of time.

____ 4. God's Word was inspired by the men who wrote it.

____ 5. It is okay to sell the Truth to whoever will pay you the most.

____ 6. Some of God's words are true.

____ 7. We are sanctified by reading Christian books.

____ 8. God's judgments will last for 1,000 years.

____ 9. God's Word is Truth for today.

____ 10. God's Word prepares you to do good works.

____ 11. You should buy wisdom, instruction and understanding.

Memory verse: John 17:17 (Day #4).

Books of Old Testament: We will also memorize the names of the books of the Old Testament by learning 6 each week for 11 weeks. This week learn: Genesis, Exodus, Leviticus, Numbers, Deuteronomy, Joshua.

Week 2

Know God's Word

Day #6   **Memorize The Word**

*Thy word have I hid in mine heart,
that I might not sin against thee.*
Psalms 119:11

Squirrels like to hide acorns so that they will have a food supply during the time of year when trees are no longer producing them. Many stories have been written about people who have hidden treasure in the ground or in a secret place in a house so they could keep it safe from those who would try to steal it from them. The Bible teaches us to hide God's Word in our hearts so that we won't sin against God. When you are tempted to do something wrong and don't have your Bible with you, those Words that are hidden in your heart will keep you from sinning. People may try to take your Bible away from you, but they can never take away God's Words that you have memorized and hidden away in your heart. Make a commitment today to memorize as many Bible verses as you can.

Prayer: *Lord Jesus, today I am asking for your help as I study Your Word and memorize scriptures that will help me to keep sin out of my life. Amen.*

 Day #7   **It Is Written**

And when the tempter came to him, he said, If thou be the Son of God, command that these stones be made bread. But he answered and said, It is written, Man shall not live by bread alone, but by every word that proceedeth out of the mouth of God.
Matthew 4:3-4

While Jesus was spending some time alone, the devil came to Him and tried to talk Him into turning rocks into pieces of bread to eat. Jesus was hungry because He had not eaten in over a month, but He refused to listen to the devil's suggestion. Instead, He quoted an Old Testament scripture to the devil. Two other times, the devil tried to talk Jesus into doing something wrong, but each time, Jesus quoted a scripture to him. The devil will talk to you and try to get you to do things that are not right. The way to make him hush is to quote a scripture back to him. It is very important to study the Bible and know what it says, so you will act right and talk right when you are tempted to do or say something wrong.

Prayer: *Lord Jesus, you gave us your Word so we would learn what was right and wrong. As I read your Word each day, help me to learn its teachings so I will choose to do what is right when I am tempted. Amen.*

 Day #8   Study To Understand

Study to shew thyself approved unto God, a workman that needeth not to be ashamed, rightly dividing the word of truth.
2 Timothy 2:15[5]

I have loved my Bible ever since I was a little girl. I read it every day and memorized dozens of scriptures. I felt certain that I could answer any question that someone could ask me concerning what I believed. However, there came a day that someone asked me to prove who Jesus is. The lady even handed me a New Testament and sarcastically said, "Prove it." Suddenly, all the dozens of scriptures I had memorized through the years left me, and I frantically turned pages in her Bible while she mocked me and said it wasn't there. My new baby started crying, and I was too distracted to think. After a few minutes, I handed the Bible back to her, picked up my baby, and left the business as the lady mockingly said, "I knew you couldn't prove it." From that day forward, I studied even harder to make sure that I would not be embarrassed the next time someone asked me to show them scriptures to prove what I believed.

Prayer: *Lord Jesus, I don't want to be embarrassed when someone asks questions about what your Word teaches. Help me to study and learn how to tell others about the words of truth found in the pages of my Bible. Amen.*

---

[5] See also: Psalms 119:6, 46, 80.

Day #9   Start Learning From Childhood

And that from a child thou hast known the holy scriptures, which are able to make thee wise unto salvation through faith which is in Christ Jesus.
2 Timothy 3:15

It is a proven fact that children can memorize and learn new information easier than adults can. Paul praised Timothy for studying the scriptures when he was a child. He said that knowledge of God's Word would give you an understanding of the salvation and faith that is found in Christ Jesus. Make up games, or save your money to purchase games that help you learn and memorize Bible verses. While you are having fun learning the Bible, the knowledge you gain will stay with you the rest of your life.

Prayer: *Lord Jesus, I am thankful for every time an adult read your Word to me before I learned to read it for myself. I love playing games and singing songs that help me to remember your Word. Thank you for helping me to understand what your Word teaches about how to be saved. Amen.*

Day #10   Be Ready To Give An Answer

But sanctify the Lord God in your hearts: and be ready always to give an answer to every man that asketh you a reason of the hope that is in you with meekness and fear.
1 Peter 3:15

Bible quizzing was one of my favorite activities when I was a young teenage girl. The youth on our team would study and memorize the chosen book for the year, and we would compete with other teams by answering questions over the selected material. We had to know the scriptures well so we could press the buzzer and answer the questions during a tournament. The knowledge I gained as a Bible quizzer prepared me for teaching Bible studies in homes and in our local jail as an adult. Learn the Word of God when you are young so that you will always have an answer to give to others who are searching for hope in Jesus.

Prayer: *Lord Jesus, thank you for your Word. My Bible is one of my favorite books, and I want to make time to read and study it every day so that I will have answers to give to people who need to hear a message of hope. Amen.*

 Week 2 Review

Complete the crossword below

Across
2. Paul wrote 2 letters to him.
5. Answers for God's Word give people ____.
6. Give this when you are asked a question.
9. Timothy studied holy scriptures as a little ____.
10. Tempted Jesus 3 times.

Down
1. Words of ____ are found in the Bible.
3. How to hide Word in your heart
4. Devil told Jesus, Turn stones into this.
7. Do this so you won't be ashamed.
8. Hide God's Word in heart; don't ____ against God.

Memory verses: Psalms 119:11 (Day #6); 2 Timothy 2:15 (Day #8).

Books of the Old Testament: Add to last week's books memorized: Judges, Ruth, 1 Samuel, 2 Samuel, 1 Kings, 2 Kings.

Week 3

Love God's Word

Psalms 119 is the longest chapter in the Bible, and the key theme of each of its 176 verses is the Word of God. The writer expressed his love and delight for God's Word 19 times in that chapter. This week we will study about loving the Word of God more than other things that may scream for your attention.

 **Day #11   Delight Yourself In God's Word**

And I will delight myself in thy commandments, which I have loved.
Psalms 119:47

When we think of the word *commandments,* we often think of Moses and the Ten Commandments. We may not realize that God gave many other commandments in His Word. In fact, the Bible talks about commandments over 300 times! The Psalmist said he took delight in God's commandments, and he loved them. If someone gave you a list of 300 rules to obey, would your first response be, "I am so delighted to have all these rules to obey. I love every one of them"? On 12 other occasions, the Psalmist writes about his great delight for God's laws.[6] What brings delight to you?

Prayer: *Lord Jesus, sometimes I get tired of being told to do this, do that; don't do this or don't do that. Help me to understand that rules are given to help me grow up to be a good citizen of my country and a mature Christian in your Kingdom. Help me to study your Word and be able to say with the Psalmist, "I delight in your commandments and love every one of them." Amen.*

 Day #12   Meditate On God's Word

O how love I thy law! it is my meditation all the day.
Psalms 119:97[7]

After Moses died, Joshua became the new leader of the children of Israel. God spoke to Joshua one day during prayer and told him to be strong and courageous as he led the people across the Jordan River into the land of Canaan. Then God reminded him to remember every law that Moses had given the people. He promised to give Joshua great success in his life if he would meditate on those laws day and night and obey them. What do you think about most often? God promises success for those who love His laws and think about them throughout the day.

---

[6] For scriptures about delighting in God's law, see also: Psalms 1:2; 37:4; 40:8; 112:1; 119:16, 24, 35, 70, 77, 92, 143, 174.
[7] For scriptures on meditation, see also: Joshua 1:1-9; Psalms 1:2; 63:6; 77:12; 119:15, 23, 48, 78, 148; 143:5; 1 Timothy 4:15.

Prayer: *Lord Jesus, I like to daydream about many things that interest me. Help me to turn my thoughts to your Word and spend more time thinking about the laws and the promises that you have given to me in those pages. Amen.*

 Day #13   God's Word Is Better Than Gold

Therefore I love thy commandments above gold; yea, above fine gold.
Psalms 119:127

Money is very attractive. Parents offer money to give you incentive to do your chores, make good grades, or learn your Bible memory verses. The Apostle Paul cautioned young Timothy against falling in love with money because it can pull you away from God and lead you away from the Truth found in His Word.[8] Although you need money to pay bills, buy food, clothes, and a place to live, you must be careful that you don't desire money so much that you miss Church or neglect prayer and study of God's Word to earn more money. Do you love God's Word more than you love earning money?

Prayer: *Lord Jesus, thank you for helping me to earn enough money to buy the things I need. Help me to value your Word more than I value earning money. Amen.*

 Day #14   God's Word Is Pure

Thy word is very pure: therefore thy servant loveth it.
Psalms 119:140

You can read God's word for hours and not encounter one inappropriate word. Every teaching in the Word is complete; no compromises or watered-down commands to make things easier to obey. No other book can match the purity of God's Word. Psalms 12:6 compares the purity of God's Word to silver that has been purified in a furnace seven times. The subject of purity is discussed almost one hundred times in the Bible. Some of the subjects discussed are: pure gold, pure frankincense, pure olive oil, pure words, pure thoughts, pure hands, and pure prayers.[9] God doesn't

---

[8] 1 Timothy 6:10. See also: Psalms 19:7-11; 119:72.
[9] See also: Psalms 19:8; Proverbs 30:5; Matthew 5:8.

want anything to be contaminated. Make sure nothing comes into your life that would cause you to lose your purity in God's sight.

Prayer: *Lord Jesus, I didn't realize that purity was such an important subject with you. Help me to check myself every day and make sure the things I read, say, and do will be appropriate and pure in your sight. Amen.*

 Day #15   **God's Word Gives Peace**

Great peace have they which love thy law: and nothing shall offend them.
Psalms 119:165

Jesus told a story about a man who sowed seed on four different kinds of ground. Then He compared the ground to different conditions of a person's heart. The seed that fell on stony ground was like a person who was excited when they first heard God's Word, but they didn't go on to learn about the things God's Word required them to do. In time they got offended at something the preacher said, and they left the church.[10] People who study God's Word and let it change them will grow deep spiritual roots, and if someone points out sin in their life, they don't get offended. They pray, repent and change. When you have that kind of love for God and His Word, nothing can offend you.

Prayer: *Lord Jesus, help my knowledge and love for your Word to grow more every day so that nothing will be able to offend me and make me walk away from serving you. Amen.*

---

[10] Matthew 13:1-23; Mark 4:1-20.

 Week 3 Review

Match the definitions on the left to the words on the right.

1. Longest chapter in Bible   ____ Offends

2. Appears 19 times in Psalms 119.   ____ Purity

3. Do this all day long.   ____ Delight

4. Mentioned in Bible over 300 times ____ Silver

5. Joshua promised this for meditating on Word. ____ Commandments

6. Don't fall in love with this.   ____ Stony

7. God's Word is very _____.   ____ Psalms 119

8. Love commandments more than metal. ____ Love, delight

9. Discussed almost 100 times in the Bible. ____ Gold

10. Nothing _____ those who love God's law. ____ Meditate

11. People whose heart is _____ get offended. ____ Money

12. Purified in a furnace 7 times.   ____ Pure

13. Subject mentioned 12 times in Psalms. ____ Success

Memory Verse: Psalms 119:165 (Day #15).

Books of the Old Testament: Add to the 12 books already learned: 1 Chronicles, 2 Chronicles, Ezra, Nehemiah, Esther, Job.

Week 4

Marriage - God's Way

Day #16   Marriage = One Man and One Woman

*And the LORD God said, It is not good that the man should be alone;
I will make him an help meet for him. And the LORD God caused a deep sleep
to fall upon Adam, and he slept: and he took one of his ribs,
and closed up the flesh instead thereof, And the rib, which the LORD God
had taken from man, made he a woman, and brought her unto the man.
And Adam said, This is now bone of my bones, and flesh of my flesh:
she shall be called Woman, because she was taken out of Man.
Therefore shall a man leave his father and his mother,
and shall cleave unto his wife: and they shall be one flesh.*
Genesis 2:18, 21-24

God established the very first home in the Garden of Eden with the creation of Adam and his wife, Eve. The pattern was forever set that marriage should consist of one man and one woman. Because Adam and Eve were the only two people on earth in the beginning, God instructed them to have children so the earth could become populated. God also told Adam that the man was to leave his family and start a brand new home with his wife. Since that time, God's plan for families has not changed. It is because of this pattern that civilizations have remained stable for thousands of years. Sometimes death, a divorce, or some other factor may create a different family structure than the Biblical pattern. If you live in a home with a different structure, don't be discouraged. God can help you grow up to be a well-adjusted young man or young woman.

Prayer: *Lord Jesus, thank you for giving us a pattern for families in the very beginning of the world. When I grow up and find the right person to marry and begin my own family, help me to follow the pattern that you started with Adam and Eve. Amen.*

Day #17   A Husband Should Love His Wife

*Husbands, love your wives, even as Christ also loved the church,
and gave himself for it; So ought men to love their wives
as their own bodies. He that loveth his wife loveth himself.*
Ephesians 5:25, 28[11]

God compares the love of a husband for his wife to the love that He had for the Church. God was willing to die so that sinners could be made clean from their sins and become a part of His bride, the Church. He said that men should have that same kind of unselfish love for their wives.

My husband was a great example of that type of love. He worked hard to provide for our family, and willingly gave up things he wanted or enjoyed so that he could provide for the desires of other members of the family. When I decided that I wanted to go back to college, he sold his big tractor and all its accessories to provide the money for my tuition. Women who receive that kind of love from their husbands feel safe in their marriage.

Prayer: *Lord Jesus, although I am too young right now to think about getting married, I thank you for the pattern for building a healthy marriage that is given in your Word. Help me to apply these teachings to my life so that if I get married when I grow up, my home will follow the pattern that is described in your Word. Amen.*

 Day #18   The Husband Is The Leader

*Wives, submit yourselves unto your own husbands, as unto the Lord.
For the husband is the head of the wife, even as Christ is the head of the church:
and he is the saviour of the body. Therefore as the church is subject unto Christ,
so let the wives be to their own husbands in every thing.*
Ephesians 5:22-24[12]

The Lord established an authority structure for Godly marriages. Just as Jesus is the head of the Church, so the husband is the head of the home. The husband is commanded to love his wife, and if he loves her the way

---

[11] Scriptures for additional study about husbands and wives: Proverbs 18:22; Colossians 3:19.
[12] Additional information on the role of a Godly wife: Proverbs 31:10-31.

Jesus loves the Church, his wife should not have difficulty in submitting to his leadership in the home. Someone has to be the boss, and God has set the pattern that the husband should lead, and his wife and children follow.

Prayer: *Lord Jesus, although I am too young to get married right now, I am thankful for the pattern you have shown me in your Word for a Godly marriage. I will pay attention to my parents and other Godly couples in our church so that I can have role models to follow when it comes time for me to marry. Amen.*

Day #19   Do Not Marry An Unbeliever

*Be ye not unequally yoked together with unbelievers:
for what fellowship hath righteousness with unrighteousness?
and what communion hath light with darkness?*
2 Corinthians 6:14

Finding a marriage partner is a very serious matter, and God's Word gives specific instructions concerning the type of person to look for. Although it is important that the boy and girl have things in common, the most important matter for building a strong marriage is the matter of being in agreement in your religious beliefs. If you disagree on spiritual matters, any children born into the home will be torn between the conflicting viewpoints of each parent. When I was a teenager, my pastor taught me that "every date was a potential mate." So don't even allow yourself to get interested in someone who is an unbeliever. Wait for God to send someone who shares your beliefs.

Prayer: *Lord Jesus, I love you so much and do not want to bring anyone into my life who would not share that same love for you. Even though I am young, prepare a special person for me who will love you wholeheartedly, and we can join our lives together to work in your Kingdom. Amen.*

Day #20   Parents Must Teach Children About God

And these words, which I command thee this day, shall be in thine heart: And thou shalt teach them diligently unto thy children, and shalt talk of them when thou sittest in thine house, and when thou walkest by the way, and when thou liest down, and when thou risest up. And thou shalt bind them for a sign upon thine hand, and they shall be as frontlets between thine eyes. And thou shalt write them upon the posts of thy house, and on thy gates.
Deuteronomy 6:6-9

Once a man and woman bring children into their home, the Bible gives them the important responsibility of teaching the children about God and His laws. Teaching about God is not only the job of a pastor or Sunday School teacher. It must also take place in the home. Moses used the word *diligently* to stress that teaching is an important part of our lifestyle. You should talk about God when you are just hanging around the house, or walking outside, or riding in the car. Talk about God when you are getting ready for bed and the first thing when you wake up in the morning. Hang scripture plaques on the walls of your home so that you have constant reminders that you are part of God's family and live according to His laws.[13]

Prayer: *Lord Jesus, help me to guard the things I say, the games I play, the things I watch, and the places I go. Let me be a good example of a Christian in my home, my school, my neighborhood, my church, and everywhere I go. When I grow up and have children of my own, I want to be "diligent" in training them to live a Godly life. Amen.*

---

[13] Training the children and grandchildren about God is commanded many times in scripture. Here are additional scriptures for further study. Deuteronomy 11:18-21; Psalms 71:17-18; 78:1-7; Titus 2:1-8.

Week 4 Review

Unscramble the following words below. Children – church - home - husband – love – man - marriage – parents – submit - unbeliever - wife – woman.

1. garimare   Marriage

2. fewi   Wife

3. shandub   _____

4. velo   _____

5. liverbunee   _____

6. spentar   _____

7. drilhenc   _____

8. ehmo   _____

9. bustim   _____

10. crcuhh   _____

11. mowna   _____

12. nma   _____

Memory Verse: Deuteronomy 6.6-9 (Day #20).

Books of the Old Testament: Add to the 18 books already learned: Psalms, Proverbs, Ecclesiastes, Song of Solomon, Isaiah, Jeremiah.

Week 5

Correction Develops Character

Jesus, help me to be a good girl.

Day #21   Obedience With A Promise

*Children, obey your parents in the Lord: for this is right.
Honour thy father and mother; (which is the first commandment with promise).*
Ephesians 6:1-2

Sometimes you might get tired of being bossed around by your parents and may say, "Why do I have to obey them?" Two reasons are given in this scripture. First of all, it is the right thing to do. Secondly, obedience and respect for your parents is the fifth commandment of the Ten Commandments, and it comes with a promise of long life.[14]

Prayer: *Lord Jesus, when I get mad at my parents for not letting me have my way, forgive me and renew my love and respect for them.*

 Day #22   Obey Parents

*Children, obey your parents in all things:
for this is well pleasing unto the Lord.*
Colossians 3:20

"Brush your teeth." "Put your toys away." "Share your toys with your sister." "Don't forget to take out the trash." "Is your homework done?" "Help me fold the clean clothes." "Make your bed before you eat breakfast."

Do you sometimes wish your parents didn't have so many rules? What if there were no rules, and everyone could do whatever they wanted to do, whenever they wanted to do it? What if mom decided she was too tired to grocery shop when there was no food in the house? What would you eat? What if no one washed the dirty dishes or the dirty clothes? What would you eat out of, or what would you wear? In order to have peace in the home, rules are necessary. What if dad quit his job because it was more fun to stay home and rest? Where would you get money to pay bills? When everyone has a job and does it well, no one is grouchy because they have to do more than someone else. Whatever house rules your parents make,

---

[14] Exodus 20:12.

obey them to the best of your ability because God is watching, and your obedience pleases Him.

Prayer: *Lord Jesus, I sometimes get angry with mom and dad because they want me to work before I play. Help me to respect their right to make the rules and obey them without showing a bad attitude. Amen.*

 Day #23   Correction Produces Wisdom

*The rod and reproof give wisdom:
but a child left to himself bringeth his mother to shame.*
Proverbs 29:15

There once was a prince in Israel whose name was Adonijah. He was a good boy most of the time, but his dad, King David, spoiled him and let him have his way all the time. As a result, he grew up to be a very selfish man. When his father was old, Prince Adonijah decided he would get some followers to make him the king, and he would kick his dad out of the palace. He almost succeeded, but the prophet, Nathan warned King David about Adonijah's plot, and David quickly made Prince Solomon the next king over Israel.[15]

The wise King Solomon later wrote that children who do not receive spankings will eventually bring embarrassment to their parents. Correction for wrongdoing will cause a child to fear the punishment and change their behavior.

Prayer: *Lord Jesus, I do not like it when my parents spank me, but I do not want to grow up and become a spoiled brat like Adonijah. Help me to accept correction and learn to be good so I won't cause shame and embarrassment to my parents.*

---

[15] 1 Kings 1:1-53

Day #24   Response to Correction

Correct thy son, and he shall give thee rest;
yea, he shall give delight unto thy soul.
Proverbs 29:17

God's Word talks about obedience over 170 times.[16] Just as God expects us to obey His laws, He also expects children to obey the rules established by parents. When rules are broken, correction must take place. Solomon taught that children who receive correction when they do wrong will learn to behave and make their parents happy. So when your parents correct you for breaking the rules, just remember that they are training you to respect and obey authority. When you have learned these lessons, you will have earned their trust and made them happy.

Prayer: *Lord Jesus, help me to understand that correction is for my good, and if I will accept it with a good attitude, I will learn to behave and make my parents happy. Amen.*

Day #25   Sibling Unity

Behold, how good and how pleasant it is for brethren to dwell together in unity!
Psalms 133:1

Nothing is more wearisome for parents than children who fuss, fight, and tattle on each other. The Bible tells us that our homes will be pleasant places to live when everyone learns to get along with each other. Do you want to have a pleasant home? Then make an extra effort to be nice to your brothers and sisters.

Prayer: *Lord Jesus, with your help, I want to make my home a pleasant place so that everyone will enjoy living here.*

---

[16] For further study on correction, see these scriptures: Proverbs 3:11; 13:24; 19:18; Hebrews 12:5-11.

Week 5 Review

Fill in the blanks with answers from this week's lessons on correction.

Children should obey their parents because it is the _____ thing to do. This commandment comes with a _____ of long _____. Obedience to _____ is well pleasing to the Lord. The _____ and _____ give wisdom, but a child who isn't corrected causes _____ to his mother. Prince _____ was very spoiled by his father, King David. He even tried to become _____ over Israel. God's Word talks about _____ over _____ times. When parents correct children for breaking the rules, they are training them to _____ and _____ authority. It is good and pleasant for brothers to live together in _____.

Memory Verse: Ephesians 6:1-2 (Day #21); Psalms 133:1 (Day #25).
Books of the Old Testament: Add to the 24 books already learned: Lamentations, Ezekiel, Daniel, Hosea, Joel, Amos.

Week 6

Wise Words From King Solomon

Day #26   Listen To Parents

My son, hear the instruction of thy father, and forsake not the law of thy mother.
Proverbs 1:8[17]

The wise King Solomon taught in two places in Proverbs that children should listen to their father's instructions and obey their mother's laws. In practical application, you might say that dads tell children what they need to do, but moms tell the children the steps they need to take to obey dad's instructions. King Solomon's son, Rehoboam, refused to listen and obey his father's wise words. Instead, he listened to the rich kids who grew up with him. Consequently, the people rebelled against his rule. Ten tribes of Israel chose another king and left unwise Rehoboam with only two tribes to rule.[18] Sometimes you may think your friends or other people have better advice for you to follow, but Godly parents know you better than anyone else. Honor them first and listen to their wise advice for your life.

Prayer: *Lord Jesus, thank you for parents who love you and do their best to teach me how to please you. When I am tempted to listen to my friends and ignore my parents, help me to remember the story of Rehoboam. I want to grow up to be the best Christian I can be. Amen.*

Day #27   Run Away From Temptation

My son, if sinners entice thee, consent thou not.
My son, walk not thou in the way with them;
refrain thy foot from their path:
For their feet run to evil, and make haste to shed blood.
Proverbs 1:10, 15-16[19]

The devil is a master at tempting people to do wrong. Temptation can come in many ways. It may be in a book, a magazine, something you see in a DVD, electronic game, or online. Solomon taught his son to walk away from anyone or anything that would tempt him to do wrong. You must make up your mind how you will avoid temptation before you are tempted, so you will already have a plan of escape. Be careful about being

---

[17] See also: Proverbs 6:20
[18] 1 Kings 12; 2 Chronicles 10.
[19] See also: Proverbs 1:10-19; 4:14-19; 1 Timothy 6:20-21.

friends with a group of people who always seem to get into trouble. You may find yourself in trouble by being friends with them, even if you don't do anything wrong. These kind of people go around looking for trouble. Don't be their friend. God will bless those who stay away from trouble.[20]

Prayer: *Lord Jesus, I want to be blessed for doing what is right. Help me to recognize things that displease you and stay away from them. Amen.*

Day #28   God Gives Correction For Wrongdoing

*My son, despise not the chastening of the LORD;
neither be weary of his correction: For whom the LORD loveth
he correcteth; even as a father the son in whom he delighteth.*
Proverbs 3:11-12[21]

Just as parents correct their children when they do wrong, so does God correct His children when they do wrong. Most of God's correction is done through the instructions that are written in His Word. When you read your Bible and realize you have done something that displeases God, it is your responsibility to say you are sorry, and change your actions. Correction is given, not to hurt you, but to develop Godly character in you. Don't become weary or resentful of correction. Accept it gratefully, and it will make you a better person.

Prayer: *Lord Jesus, correction sometimes embarrasses me, especially if it is done when others are present. Help me to accept correction, and let it change me into the person you want me to be. Amen.*

Day #29   Obedience Brings Long Life

Hear, O my son, and receive my sayings; and the years of thy life shall be many.
Proverbs 4:10

If you want to live a long time, pay attention to the teachings of your parents. They will teach you how to choose healthy foods and how to keep your body clean. They will teach you to wear proper clothes in the cold

---

[20] Psalms 1:1-6
[21] Hebrews 12:5.

and heat so you won't get sick. They will teach you to avoid substances that cause diseases that may shorten your life. They will teach you to work and exercise your body so it will become strong. Moses also taught that respect and honor for your parents would give you a long life. Of course, accidents can happen that will shorten your time on earth, but obedience to the teachings of your parents about living a healthy life will result in a longer, more satisfying one.

Prayer: *Lord Jesus, I want to live a healthy life, so help me to obey the teachings I receive concerning how to take care of my body. Amen.*

Day #30   Happy Parents

My son, if thine heart be wise, my heart shall rejoice, even mine.
Proverbs 23:15[22]

Do you want to make your parents happy? Solomon says that wise children cause their parents to rejoice. It isn't enough to fill your head with lots of facts and information, for knowledge alone won't bring rejoicing to your parents. Knowledge must be combined with the wisdom that teaches you how to use knowledge. For example: knowledge teaches you that you may cross a street in a pedestrian walkway, but wisdom teaches you to look both ways and make sure the traffic light is green, or that no traffic is coming. Children who have acquired the wisdom to apply what they have been taught will bring great joy to their parents.

Prayer: *Lord Jesus, my parents have spent much time and money in raising me and giving me an education. Help me to make them proud of me by learning how to use all this knowledge to become a wise young person and adult. Amen.*

---

[22] See also: Proverbs 10:1; 15:20; 23:24-25; 27;11.

Week 6 Review

Find the following words in the grid below.

Advice - Bible - character - children - correction - education - escape - exercise - happy - healthy - heart - honor - knowledge - Moses - obedience - parents - Rehoboam - rejoice - Solomon - temptation.

S	Q	A	K	O	Q	T	C	Q	H	E	A	L	T	H	Y
T	I	D	F	T	Q	E	E	O	K	Q	S	W	I	X	W
N	T	V	D	Y	P	C	S	M	L	B	I	B	L	E	Y
E	S	I	D	V	I	F	F	G	P	H	A	P	P	Y	N
R	O	C	T	D	E	D	U	C	A	T	I	O	N	C	M
A	S	E	T	D	R	E	T	C	A	R	A	H	C	O	N
P	E	C	N	E	I	D	E	B	O	L	Y	T	S	O	S
O	K	N	O	W	L	E	D	G	E	D	B	E	I	F	Y
N	Z	H	O	Q	M	Q	L	B	B	F	S	T	Y	O	U
S	R	F	H	E	A	R	T	D	F	C	C	A	H	E	N
I	E	N	S	E	O	S	O	R	A	E	W	O	Y	N	K
V	J	J	N	D	B	J	K	P	R	K	N	C	X	G	F
X	O	H	S	J	O	G	E	R	N	O	M	O	L	O	S
R	I	D	F	K	H	Y	O	H	R	B	S	S	E	R	D
N	C	R	N	Q	E	C	L	E	X	E	R	C	I	S	E
K	E	V	N	E	R	D	L	I	H	C	G	M	R	I	T

Memory Verse: Proverbs 1:8 (Day #26).

Books of the Old Testament: Add to the 30 books already learned: Obadiah, Jonah, Micah, Nahum, Habakkuk, Zephaniah.

Week 7

Old Testament Heroes

Day #31   Rebekah

And he said O LORD God of my master Abraham… And let it come to pass, that the damsel to whom I shall say, Let down thy pitcher, I pray thee, that I may drink; and she shall say, Drink, and I will give thy camels drink also: let the same be she that thou hast appointed for thy servant Isaac; and thereby shall I know that thou hast shewed kindness unto my master.
Genesis 24:12, 14

When Isaac grew up, his dad Abraham decided it was time to find a wife for him. In those days, the parents often selected the bride for their sons. So Abraham sent Eliezer, who was a trusted servant, to his brother's house to see if there were any daughters who would be willing to move to Canaan and marry Isaac. After arriving, Eliezer asked God to help him find the right girl by giving him a sign. He said if he asked a girl for a drink, and she offered to give drinks to all his camels, then he would know that she was the one God had chosen. Rebekah was the first girl to come to the well, and when he asked her for a drink, she immediately drew water for him and volunteered to draw water for all his camels also. He asked her about her family and discovered that God had led him right to Abraham's family. Rebekah took him to her house, and Eliezer asked if he could take Rebekah back to Canaan to marry Isaac.

When Rebekah went to the well that day, she didn't realize that her unselfish act of drawing many pitchers of water for the thirsty camels would result in her going away to marry the man God had chosen for her. Whenever you are asked to do something, do it to the best of your ability, and do even more than you are asked to do. You never know what kind of blessing God has in store for you when you cheerfully do more than is required.

Prayer: *Lord Jesus, I don't know what blessings you have prepared for me today. Help me to do all my work with a good attitude and then look for ways that I can do other things that I have not been asked to do. Amen.*

Day #32   Jacob

And Jacob was left alone; and there wrestled a man with him until the breaking of the day. And when he saw that he prevailed not against him, he touched the hollow of his thigh; and the hollow of Jacob's thigh was out of joint, as he wrestled with him. And he said, Thy name shall be called no more Jacob, but Israel: for as a prince hast thou power with God and with men, and hast prevailed.
Genesis 32:24-25, 28

Jacob was the younger son of twin boys born to Isaac and Rebekah. His older brother, Esau, loved to hunt and spend time outdoors, but Jacob was just the opposite. He enjoyed staying in the tent with his mother and learning how to cook special foods with her. Jacob's name means cheater, and he lived up to that name when he bargained with Esau for the family birthright and years later, he tricked his blind dad into giving him the family blessing which was supposed to be given to Esau. When Esau threatened to kill him, Jacob fled the country. During his journey to his Uncle Laban's home, he had an encounter with God through a dream about a ladder going to Heaven. He named the place Bethel and promised to serve the God of his fathers and give tithes of all his income to God.[23] After arriving in Haran, Jacob met and eventually married both of Uncle Laban's daughters. Their names were Leah and Rachel. Laban played several tricks on Jacob during the 20 years he lived in that area. Finally, Jacob decided to take his family back to Canaan, but he received news on the way that Esau was coming after him with a large group of men. Jacob spent a whole night in desperate prayer for God to bless him. At the end of the night, Jacob received a blessing, and his name was changed to Israel. No longer did he have to wear the name of deceiver and cheater. From that day forward, Jacob was a changed man who became known as a prince who had power with God.

Maybe you have done things that you are ashamed of, but you can confess those sins to God, and He will forgive you and make you a new person.

Prayer: *Lord Jesus, when I do something hurtful or mean to someone, help me to remember the story of Jacob and repent of my wrongs. You have a blessing for those who want to follow you and live according to your laws, and I want to receive that blessing for my life. Amen.*

---

[23] Genesis 28:10-22

Day #33   Joseph

And Pharaoh said unto Joseph, See, I have set thee over all the land of Egypt. And Pharaoh took off his ring from his hand, and put it upon Joseph's hand, and arrayed him in vestures of fine linen, and put a gold chain about his neck; And he made him to ride in the second chariot which he had; and they cried before him, Bow the knee: and he made him ruler over all the land of Egypt.
Genesis 41:41-43

Joseph was the eleventh of twelve sons born to Jacob. His mother's name was Rachel. Jacob spoiled Joseph and gave him a beautiful coat made of many colors. When Joseph was very young, he had two dreams about ruling over his parents and brothers. Joseph's brothers were jealous of him because of his dreams and because he was their dad's favorite son. One day when Joseph was seventeen, his angry brothers sold him to some Ishmaelite merchants, and they let their dad believe he had been killed by a wild animal. Joseph was taken to Egypt and sold as a slave to an army captain named Potiphar. God was with Joseph, and Potiphar placed Joseph in charge of his household business. One day Potiphar's wife told a lie about Joseph, and he was put in prison. The jailer recognized God's hand on Joseph's life, and he put him in charge of all the prisoners. Joseph even interpreted dreams for two of the prisoners. After years in prison, the day came that Pharaoh had a dream, and Joseph was brought out of prison to interpret the dream. Pharaoh recognized God's wisdom in Joseph and at thirty years of age, Joseph was appointed as the second ruler of the land. Joseph oversaw the storage of food during seven years of plentiful harvests, and during the seven years of famine he sold the stored food to the Egyptians and others who needed it. Joseph's brothers came to buy food in Egypt, and when they bowed before Joseph, he remembered the two dreams he had when he was a young boy. Joseph gave food to his brothers, and later, his entire family moved to Egypt. Jacob saw Joseph again, and they were together for the remainder of their lives.[24]

Even though Joseph was given special favors at times when he was young, he loved God, and kept a good attitude after his brothers sold him into slavery. God protected him and promoted him to be a ruler over Egypt. God has plans for your life. Sometimes He allows you to be mistreated and

---

[24] For more information about the life of Joseph, read: Genesis 30:22-24; chapters 37, 39-50.

lied about, but if you can keep a good attitude through all the hard times in life, God will work everything out according to His plans for you.

Prayer: *Lord Jesus, when people tell lies about me and get me in trouble, help me to remember the story of Joseph and keep a good attitude through it all. Amen.*

Day #34   Moses

By faith Moses, when he was born, was hid three months of his parents, because they saw he was a proper child; and they were not afraid of the king's commandment. By faith Moses, when he was come to years, refused to be called the son of Pharaoh's daughter; Choosing rather to suffer affliction with the people of God, than to enjoy the pleasures of sin for a season;
Hebrews 11:23-25

Moses was born in Egypt during a time when Pharaoh had made slaves of all the Israelites who lived there. Pharaoh was afraid the Israelites would become strong, and fight against the Egyptians, so he made a law that all the boy babies born to Israelite families were to be thrown into the Nile River and drowned. Moses' parents hid their new baby for three months, but when he got too big to hide, Moses' mother, Jochebed, made him a little bed in a waterproof basket. Then she put Moses in the basket and set it in the Nile River. Moses' sister, Miriam stood by the river to see what would happen to her little brother. Soon the princess came to wash in the water, and she found the little basket. When she opened the lid, Moses began to cry. She felt sorry for him and decided to keep him as her own son. Miriam bravely stepped up and asked if the princess would like someone to nurse the baby, and the princess said yes. So Moses' mother was given permission to nurse and take care of her own baby for several years, and she even got paid to do it. Jochebed did such a good job of teaching Moses about God that in spite of all the wealth and Egyptian education that was given him, Moses never forgot that he was an Israelite who worshiped only one God. When he was grown, he left his position to be the next king of Egypt, and God chose him to be the leader of the Israelites for 40 years. God even gave Moses the Ten Commandments so he could teach them to the Israelites.[25]

---

[25] Exodus 2-3.

The things you learn about God when you are young will stay in your heart all your life, and God uses children who desire to do what He says.

Prayer: *Lord Jesus, help me to choose the Christian way of life instead of the way of the world. I know you have big plans for me, and I want to be obedient to your Word so I can accomplish what you have called me to do. Amen.*

Day #35   Miriam

And Miriam the prophetess, the sister of Aaron, took a timbrel in her hand; and all the women went out after her with timbrels and with dances. And Miriam answered them, Sing ye to the LORD, for he hath triumphed gloriously; the horse and his rider hath he thrown into the sea.
Exodus 15:20-21

Miriam was the oldest child of Amram and Jochebed. She had two younger brothers named Aaron and Moses. When her baby brother, Moses was in danger of being killed, she watched over his little basket in the Nile River. When he was found by the princess, Miriam bravely asked if she could get a nurse to take care of the baby for her. Many years later, when her brothers, Moses and Aaron, had successfully led several million Israelites out of Egypt and across the Red Sea, Miriam got out her tambourine and led the women in songs of praise and dances to God for delivering them from the Egyptians. The Bible also says that she was a prophetess. That means that God used her to speak words of inspiration and encouragement to the people. God is looking for girls who are helpful to others, and speak kind words to people who are sad. God also needs worshipers who will lead others in singing songs of praise to Him. If you enjoy singing or playing a musical instrument, God wants to use those gifts in the Church. Practice and always do your best.

Prayer: *Lord Jesus, I love to sing songs of praise to you. I offer myself and my gift back to you. Use me to be an enthusiastic worshiper in the Church. Amen.*

Week 7 Review

Fill in the blanks for the questions.

Rebekah was chosen to be the wife of _____ because she offered to give a _____ to Eliezer's _____.

Jacob had a brother named _____. Jacob's name meant _____.

Jacob's parents were _____ and _____. He bargained with Esau for the family _____, and he tricked his dad into giving him the family _____. Jacob's wives were _____ and _____. Jacob's name was changed to _____.

Joseph had ____ brothers, and his mother's name was _____. Joseph's dad gave him a beautiful _____. Joseph's brothers sold him, and he became a slave and a prisoner in _____. Joseph was _____ years old when he became a ruler in Egypt. He remembered his dreams when his brothers _____ before him.

Miriam's parents were _____ and _____. After Israel crossed the _____ Sea, Miriam used her _____ to lead the women in singing praises to God.

Pharaoh made a law that all newborn boy babies had to be thrown into the _____ River. Jochebed hid her baby boy for ___ months. Then she put Moses into a _____ and set him in the Nile River. _____ watched the basket until it was found by the _____. God gave the _____ Commandments to Moses.

Memory Verse: Hebrews 11:23-25 (Day #34).

Books of the Old & New Testament: Add to the 36 books already learned: Haggai, Zechariah, Malachi, Matthew, Mark, Luke.

Week 8

Ten Commandments

Day #36   First and Second Commandments

Thou shalt have no other gods before me.
Thou shalt not make unto thee any graven image...
Exodus 20:3-4

The Ten Commandments that God gave to Moses have been printed and framed in pictures in homes and government buildings. They have been carved in stone and placed as monuments in parks and on government property.

In the First Commandment, God makes it very plain that He wants to be your God, and He doesn't want you worshiping anything or anyone beside Him.

In the Second Commandment, He forbids carving or creating any kind of image to worship instead of Him. He created you, and He does not want to share your worship with false gods.

Prayer: *Lord Jesus, I am thankful that you are my Creator and my God. I want to always please you with my worship and never allow anything or anyone to influence me to worship a false god. Amen.*

Day #37   Third and Fourth Commandments

Thou shalt not take the name of the LORD thy God in vain;
for the LORD will not hold him guiltless that taketh his name in vain.
Remember the sabbath day, to keep it holy.
Exodus 20:7-8

The Third Commandment instructs you to respect God's Name and never use His Name or any titles referring to Him in a disrespectful way, for God will punish those who do this.

The Fourth Commandment says that the Sabbath day is a holy day. You should set aside a day to rest, go to Church, hear God's Word taught, and worship with God's people. Even God rested on the seventh day after He had worked for six days creating the universe and everything in it.

Prayer: *Lord Jesus, your Name is holy, and I want to remember to think about the words I say so you will never be dishonored by my words. Help me to be faithful in setting aside one day of each week to focus on you and worship with your people. Amen.*

Day #38   Fifth and Sixth Commandments

Honour thy father and thy mother: that thy days may be long upon the land which the LORD *thy God giveth thee.*
Thou shalt not kill.
Exodus 20:12-13

The Fifth Commandment teaches you to show respect and courtesy to your parents. That includes responding to their instructions with the polite words of "Yes ma'am," "Yes sir," "No ma'am," and "No sir." It also includes using the word "Please" when making a request of them, and the words, "Thank you" when they give you something or do something special for you. Honoring your parents even when you don't agree with them pleases God and comes with a promise of long life.

The Sixth Commandment teaches that killing others is a sin. All human life is precious in God's eyes, and taking someone's life is a very serious offense to God.

Prayer: *Lord Jesus, sometimes it is hard for me to say nice words to my parents when they correct my behavior and hurt my feelings. Help me to remember that you are pleased when I honor my parents with my behavior and my words. I am sad when I hear about shootings and war in the news. Help people to understand that life is precious and that we should treat others who don't agree with us in the same way we would like to be treated. Amen.*

Day #39   Seventh and Eighth Commandments

Thou shalt not commit adultery.
Thou shalt not steal.
Exodus 20:14-15

The Seventh Commandment teaches that marriage and family are very important to God. Husbands and wives should be faithful to each other and not spend time with the opposite sex without their spouse being present. Marriage is sacred, and when those vows are taken, the marriage should last as long as they both live.

The Eighth Commandment forbids taking something from others that does not belong to you without their permission. Taking something you see in a store and slipping it in your pocket without paying for it is stealing. If you find a quarter in the couch cushions at your grandparents' house, you should ask if you may keep it before you stick it in your pocket. If you are playing with a friend's toy and you break it, you have stolen their enjoyment of that toy unless you buy them another one. God wants you to respect things that belong to others and not destroy them or take what does not belong to you.

Prayer: *Lord Jesus, I thank you for my parents and the home and benefits they work hard to give to me. I pray for boys and girls who have lost a parent through death, divorce, or some other situation. Please comfort the children who live in troubled homes and families. Also I thank you for all the toys and possessions I have been given. Help me to remember that someone worked hard to give me these things, and I don't ever want to take something that does not belong to me. Help me to always be honest in my dealings with others. Amen.*

Day #40 Ninth and Tenth Commandments

> *Thou shalt not bear false witness against thy neighbour.*
> *Thou shalt not covet…any thing that is thy neighbour's.*
> Exodus 20:16-17

The Ninth Commandment teaches that you should not tell lies about other people. Once you tell a lie about someone, others will believe it and think bad thoughts about the person. Your lie could ruin their reputation with others who do not know them very well. Be kind to others, and always speak the Truth.

The Tenth Commandment teaches that you should not be jealous about the things that other people have to the point that you will do anything you can to get what they have. The Apostle Paul taught young Timothy that if he had enough food to eat and enough clothes to wear, he should be content.[26] Don't beg your parents or grandparents to buy you *stuff* you do not need just because some of your friends have it. Learn to be thankful and content with the things you have.

Prayer: *Lord Jesus, help me to guard my mouth and say only true words about others, and when I see my friends getting toys, games, or clothes that I don't have, help me to be happy for them and thankful for the things I do have. Amen.*

---

[26] 1 Timothy 6:8. Also see Hebrews 13:5.

Week 8 Review

Match the definitions on the left to the words on the right.

1. Don't desire what belongs to others.   _____ 7th Command

2. Received commandments from God.   _____ 1st Command

3. Do not tell lies.   _____ 10th Command

4. Do not worship other gods.   _____ 5th Command

5. Do not steal.   _____ Moses

6. Do not worship idols.   _____ 9th Command

7. Do not commit adultery.   _____ 2nd Command

8. Honor father and mother.   _____ 3rd Command

9. Do not take God's name in vain.   _____ 8th Command

10. Do not kill.   _____ 4th Command

11. Keep the Sabbath day holy.   _____ 6th Command

Memory Verse: Exodus 20:12 (Day #38).

Books of the Old & New Testament: Add to the 42 books already learned: John, Acts, Romans, 1 Corinthians, 2 Corinthians, Galatians.

The Ten Commandments

From Ex. 20:1-17
Pam Eddings

If we would please Jesus each and ev-ry day, We'd keep His com-mand-ments so we won't go a-stray. Thou shalt have no o-ther gods be- fore Me. Thou shalt not make a grav-en i-mage. Thou shalt not take the name of God in vain. Re-mem-ber the Sab-bath, keep it ho-ly. Hon-our thy fa-ther and thy mo-ther. Thou shalt not kill, com-mit a-dul-ter-y or steal. Nei-ther shalt thou bear false wit-ness a-gainst thy neigh-bor Or cov-et any-thing that is thy neigh-bor's.

Week 9

More Old Testament Heroes

King Josiah

Day #41   Samuel

And the LORD…called,…Samuel, Samuel. Then Samuel answered, Speak; for thy servant heareth. And Samuel grew, and the LORD was with him…And all Israel from Dan even to Beersheba knew that Samuel was established to be a prophet of the LORD.
1 Samuel 3:10, 19-20

The Bible tells of a lady named Hannah, who prayed desperately for God to give her a son. She even promised to give him back to the Lord for life-long service. God granted her request, and Samuel was born. When he was a very small child, Hannah and her husband, Elkanah, brought him to live with Eli, the elderly priest. I can't imagine how difficult it must have been for Hannah to keep her promise to the Lord and leave her small son with the priest. Eli taught Samuel how to offer sacrifices and take care of the duties in the Tabernacle. Every year when Samuel's parents came to worship, his mother would bring him a coat that she had made for him. One night God called young Samuel by name and told him some things that would soon be happening to Eli's family. Everyone who came to the Tabernacle to worship recognized that Samuel had God's anointing on his life, and they knew that he would be the next judge after Eli died. Samuel did judge Israel for many years, but when he grew old, the people asked for a king like the nations around them. God granted their request, and Samuel anointed the first two kings over Israel.[27]

Samuel became an anointed and respected leader in Israel because of his mother's prayer and promise to give her son back to God for as long as he lived. God has a plan to your life also, and praying parents play a huge part in seeing God's plan unfold in your life.

Prayer: *Lord Jesus, I am thankful for parents who pray for me and teach me to love you and be obedient to your Word. Even though I am young, I want to listen to your voice as you lead me in the path you have chosen for me. Amen.*

---

[27] 1 Samuel 1-3, 9-10, 16.

Day #42   Joash

Joash was seven years old when he began to reign, and he reigned forty years in Jerusalem... And Joash did that which was right in the sight of the LORD all the days of Jehoiada the priest.
2 Chronicles 24:1-2

When Joash was just a baby, his father, King Ahaziah, died after being king for only one year. Ahaziah's mother, Athaliah, wanted to become queen, so she had all of Ahaziah's children killed except for baby Joash. Athaliah's daughter, Jehosheba, and her husband, Jehoiada, the priest, took baby Joash and hid him for six years. During that time, the wicked Queen Athaliah reigned over Judah. When Joash was seven years old, Jehoiada arranged to have him crowned king, and Queen Athaliah was executed. Joash served God as long as his Uncle Jehoiada was alive, but his heart wasn't totally committed to God. He had the Temple repaired, but he allowed the groves and temples of heathen gods to remain in the land. When Jehoiada died, some idol worshippers came and talked Joash into forsaking his worship of the true God of Israel. When his cousin, Zechariah, rebuked him for following idols, Joash became angry and had his cousin executed. Joash did not appreciate the kindness of his aunt and uncle in saving his life and teaching him the ways of God. Finally, his own servants rose against him and killed him.[28]

Joash's story shows us that sometimes people do what is right as long as they are being watched, but when that person is gone, they quickly make a change of direction and do the wrong things. It is important that you follow God because you love Him, and not because you are trying to please someone.

Prayer: *Lord Jesus, would you search my heart and see if there is any desire for things that would pull me away from you? If you find anything in my heart, please tear it out. I want more than anything to please you. Amen.*

---

[28] More information about Joash can be found in these chapters: 2 Kings 11-12 and 2 Chronicles 22-24.

Day #43   Josiah

Josiah was eight years old when he began to reign, and he reigned thirty and one years in Jerusalem… And he did that which was right in the sight of the LORD, and walked in all the way of David his father, and turned not aside to the right hand or to the left.
2 Kings 22:1-2

Josiah's dad, King Amon, had angered God because he worshiped idols. King Amon died when he was only twenty-four years old. Eight-year-old Josiah was crowned king in his father's place. Although Josiah was only a boy when he became king, he made up his mind that he would not follow his dad's false gods. Instead, he chose to ask advice from the priest, Hilkiah, and he followed his instructions throughout his life. Many changes were made in the nation while Josiah was king. He told the priests and Levites to remove anything from God's Temple that was used in idol worship, and they built a big bonfire and burned all of it. He then went through the country and tore down every altar and temple that had been built to Baal and other false gods, and burned every one of them. He also sent all the fortune-tellers and magicians out of the country. Then in the eighteenth year of his reign, the nation celebrated the greatest Passover that had ever been celebrated. God was very pleased with Josiah. During his thirty-one year reign, he single-handedly turned the nation of Israel from idolatry to the worship of the true God.[29]

You may think you are just a young child and can't do great things in an adult world, but Josiah is a great example of what one child can do to change his world when he puts his trust in God and lives according to God's laws.

Prayer: *Lord Jesus, sometimes I feel so small and unable to make a difference in the sinful world that surrounds me. Help me to remember Josiah and be an example to everyone around me. Amen.*

---

[29] Further reading about Josiah can be found in 2 Kings 21-23 and 2 Chronicles 33-35.

Day #44   Daniel

But Daniel purposed in his heart that he would not defile himself
with the portion of the king's meat, nor with the wine which he drank…
And the king communed with them; and among them all was found none like
Daniel, Hananiah, Mishael, and Azariah: therefore stood they before the king.
And in all matters of wisdom and understanding, that the king
enquired of them, he found them ten times better than all the
magicians and astrologers that were in all his realm.
Daniel 1:8, 19-20

Daniel and his three friends, Hananiah, Mishael, and Azariah were captured by the Babylonians and carried away from their homes in Judah. King Nebuchadnezzar wanted to teach some of the young men the language and customs of his country, so he selected some of them and arranged to feed them some of the best food from the king's table. Daniel and his friends were in a foreign country, away from the watchful eyes of their parents and the priests, so they could have eaten food that was forbidden in the Jewish food laws. But they decided that they would not eat anything that was forbidden. They were given permission to eat vegetables and water, and when they finally stood before King Nebuchadnezzar, they were ten times smarter than all his other advisors. They were promoted to high positions in the kingdom.

Years later Daniel was put in a den of lions because he refused to pray to King Darius instead of his God. God miraculously protected him from harm during the night he spent among the lions.[30] Because of Daniel's faithful obedience to God's laws even in a foreign country, God showed him many prophecies about the end of this age, and he wrote them down in the Bible book that bears his name.

God is looking for young men and women who will be true to Him and the teachings of the Bible even when no one is around to know if they disobey or not. God has great rewards available for those who love Him and obey His Word.

Prayer: *Lord Jesus, help me to be true to you and your Word even if no one is around to check up on me. Amen.*

---

[30] Daniel 6.

Day #45   Shadrach, Meshach, and Abednego

Shadrach, Meshach, and Abednego, answered and said to the king, O Nebuchadnezzar, we are not careful to answer thee in this matter. If it be so, our God whom we serve is able to deliver us from the burning fiery furnace, and he will deliver us out of thine hand, O king. But if not, be it known unto thee, O king, that we will not serve thy gods, nor worship the golden image which thou hast set up.
Daniel 3:16-18

King Nebuchadnezzar built a huge image and made a law that everyone had to come and bow down to the image. Even though Shadrach, Meshach, and Abednego were far away from their home and the Temple in Israel, they remembered that the second commandment in the Ten Commandments said that they were not to worship any idols; so they refused to bow down. King Nebuchadnezzar became very angry when they disobeyed his order, and he commanded that they be thrown into a very hot fiery furnace. The threat of being burned to death did not change the boys' minds. They were willing to die to obey God's laws. They were thrown into the fire, and God met them in the fire and protected them. They walked out of the fire without one burn on them, and their clothes didn't even smell like smoke. After seeing that miracle, the king made a new law that everyone had to worship the God of Shadrach, Meshach, and Abednego.

Are you willing to obey God's Word even if it means you might be put in prison or killed for your faith?

Prayer: *Lord Jesus, I love you, and I love your Word. Help me to obey your Word even if it means I could be punished or killed for it. I trust you with my life. Amen.*

Week 9 Review

Find the following words in the grid below.

Abednego - Athaliah - Azariah - Daniel - Eli - Furnace - Hananiah - Hannah - Hilkiah - Israel - Jehoiada - Jehosheba - Joash - Josiah - Judge - Lions - Meshach - Mishael - Nebuchadnezzar - Passover - Priest - Queen - Samuel - Shadrach - Tabernacle

Y	J	D	A	R	E	V	O	S	S	A	P	V	H	M
L	W	Z	D	A	W	N	D	Z	L	X	P	S	L	N
B	A	J	A	H	T	H	T	M	D	E	A	R	E	K
V	B	Z	I	I	K	X	C	N	E	O	I	B	L	M
J	E	H	O	S	H	E	B	A	J	S	U	N	V	L
L	D	G	H	R	A	J	H	L	R	C	H	H	A	Q
B	N	X	E	A	B	T	E	A	H	D	A	A	U	D
K	E	G	J	E	A	A	H	A	N	N	A	E	C	H
J	G	F	Z	L	H	Z	D	A	A	N	E	H	A	H
D	O	W	U	S	L	N	A	N	L	N	A	I	S	S
J	X	S	I	R	E	E	I	R	N	I	K	H	N	E
K	U	M	I	Z	N	A	U	M	I	L	A	O	A	L
M	N	D	Z	A	H	A	R	M	I	A	I	H	G	I
J	K	A	G	L	H	M	C	H	A	L	H	R	N	T
Y	R	J	D	E	R	G	G	E	T	S	R	N	M	V
E	L	C	A	N	R	E	B	A	T	S	E	I	R	P

Memory Verse: Daniel 3:16-18 (Day #45).

Books of the Old & New Testament: Add to the 48 books already learned: Ephesians, Philippians, Colossians, 1 Thessalonians, 2 Thessalonians, 1 Timothy.

Week 10

David - God's Boy

Day #46   David, The Shepherd

And David said unto Saul, Thy servant kept his father's sheep, and there came a lion, and a bear, and took a lamb out of the flock: And I went out after him, and smote him, and delivered it out of his mouth: and when he arose against me, I caught him by his beard, and smote him, and slew him. Thy servant slew both the lion and the bear...
1 Samuel 17:34-36

David was the youngest of Jesse's eight sons. As a young boy, his job was to spend hours and days alone while watching his father's sheep. Even though he was alone, he knew that God was always with him. He had his slingshot for a weapon against wild animals, and he practiced until he became very skilled in using it. One time he killed a lion that was attacking his sheep, and another time he killed a bear that tried to attack his sheep. During those lonely days, he also played beautiful music to God on his harp. Many of the psalms are songs that were written by David. Young children who love God can also do big things just like David did.

Prayer: *Lord Jesus, although I am not grown up yet, you have given me special talents, and I want to practice and do my best with what you have given me. I am eager to be of service to you, my family, my church, and my community. Amen.*

Day #47   David and Goliath

Then said David to the Philistine, Thou comest to me with a sword, and with a spear, and with a shield: but I come to thee in the name of the LORD of hosts, the God of the armies of Israel, whom thou hast defied. So David prevailed over the Philistine with a sling and with a stone, and smote the Philistine, and slew him; but there was no sword in the hand of David.
1 Samuel 17:45, 50

The Philistines had started a war with Israel, and David's three brothers, Eliab, Abinadab, and Shammah had been called to fight in King Saul's army. The Philistines had a giant named Goliath in their army, and for forty days, he kept challenging the Israelites to send a man to fight him. All the Israelites, including King Saul, were too terrified to accept Goliath's challenge until David arrived to bring some food to his brothers. He was angry that the giant would dare to mock the God of Israel, so he volunteered to fight him. Taking his slingshot and five stones in his bag, he marched out to meet Goliath. When Goliath saw how young David was, he mocked him and said he would feed David's flesh to the birds and animals of the field. David was not afraid. He said that he was fighting in the name of the LORD of hosts. He put one stone in his sling and with perfect accuracy, the stone hit Goliath in the head and knocked him to the ground. David became an overnight hero in Israel for his bravery.

You too can become a hero for God when you bravely stand up to bullies who mock your God and make fun of you and others for being a Christian.

Prayer: *Lord Jesus, I do not like it when a bully makes fun of me or my friends for being a Christian. Help me to bravely stand up to him and rebuke him in Jesus' name. Amen.*

Day #48   David Became King Of Israel

*And David behaved himself wisely in all his ways;
and the LORD was with him.*
1 Samuel 18:14

Several years after Saul became the first king of Israel, he became very proud and wouldn't listen to advice from the prophet, Samuel. God became angry with Saul and told Samuel to go and anoint another man to be the next king of Israel. Samuel went to David's house and after all seven of David's older brothers were passed over, David was chosen, and Samuel poured oil on his head to show that he was God's chosen man to rule Israel.[31] Although David was anointed when he was a young boy, it was many years before he became the second king of Israel. He married one of King Saul's daughters and was able to learn how the country was ruled until Saul became jealous of him. Then he had to flee for his life until King Saul was killed in battle. David was thirty years old when he became king, and he ruled Israel for forty years. During all the years he waited to become king, he behaved himself wisely and kept a good attitude even when Saul was trying to kill him. Because of his behavior, God was with him and protected him from harm.

---

[31] To read the story of David being anoint as king, go to: 1 Samuel 16:1-13.

God may put a dream in your heart when you are just a child, but it may take years for that dream to come true. Just keep a good attitude and love God, and in time, God will bring it to pass.

Prayer: *Lord Jesus, there are so many things I would like to do when I grow up, and it is hard for me to wait until I'm old enough to do them. Help me to do the things I am old enough to do now while I wait for my dreams to come true. Amen.*

Day #49   Man After God's Heart

And when he had removed [Saul], he raised up unto them David to be their king; to whom also he gave their testimony, and said, I have found David the son of Jesse, a man after mine own heart, which shall fulfil all my will.
Acts 13:22

David is one of the most well-known names in the Bible; his name occurs 895 times. Many things come to mind when we think about David. We remember him as a shepherd boy and as the hero who fought Goliath. He played beautiful music on his harp, and we love reading the many psalms that he wrote. His writings taught us much about praising God. He was the well-loved second king of Israel, and he brought music and singing into the worship at the Tabernacle. Luke wrote in Acts that David was a man after God's own heart, and God trusted David to obey all His will. Does that mean David was a perfect man? Not by a long shot. He told lies to a priest when he was running from King Saul, and he pretended to be crazy when his life was threatened by a Philistine king. He fell in love with another man's wife and had her husband killed in battle so he could marry her. If David did so many bad things in his life, why was he called a man after God's own heart? The answer lies in David's desire to repent quickly and sincerely when he did something wrong. He never blamed someone else for the wrongs he did. When the prophet confronted him and told him he had sinned, David fell on his knees and begged God to forgive him. One of David's most beautiful prayers of repentance is in Psalms 51.

Do you want to be a young man or young lady after God's own heart? The secret to finding that special place with God is to accept responsibility for all your sins, and repent often. David taught that God is near to those who admit their wrongs and repent of them.[32]

Prayer: *Lord Jesus, it is a huge relief to know that even David had many faults and made bad choices at times in his life. Sometimes I feel like such a failure when I do something I shouldn't do. Help me to have a heart like David and be quick to admit when I've done wrong and ask for forgiveness. Amen.*

Day #50   Beloved 23rd Psalm

¹ The LORD is my shepherd; I shall not want.
² He maketh me to lie down in green pastures: he leadeth me beside the still waters.
³ He restoreth my soul: he leadeth me in the paths
of righteousness for his name's sake.
⁴ Yea, though I walk through the valley of the shadow of death, I will fear no evil:
for thou art with me; thy rod and thy staff they comfort me.
⁵ Thou preparest a table before me in the presence of mine enemies:
thou anointest my head with oil; my cup runneth over.
⁶ Surely goodness and mercy shall follow me all the days of my life:
and I will dwell in the house of the LORD for ever.
Psalms 23:1-6

David was the author of Psalms 23, and it is one of the most loved and memorized chapters in the whole Bible. My aunt helped me to memorize this Psalm when I was five years old. I also taught it to my oldest grandson when he was five years old. It is comforting to know that, because God is our shepherd, He promises to take care of all our needs of rest, proper food, protection from enemies, correction when we do wrong, and spiritual growth. If you haven't memorized this chapter, today would be a good day to start hiding these promises in your heart.

Prayer: *Lord Jesus, I am thankful that you are my shepherd and that I can bring all my needs to you with the assurance that you will take care of me because I belong to you. I take comfort in being one of your sheep. Amen.*

---

[32] Psalms 34:18

Week 10 Review

Answer True or False for each statement below.

_____ 1. David killed a lion and a tiger.

_____ 2. David was the oldest of Jesse's eight sons.

_____ 3. David wrote many psalms while watching his father's sheep.

_____ 4. Two of David's brothers fought in King Saul's army.

_____ 5. Goliath was a giant in the Assyrian army.

_____ 6. David killed Goliath with his sling and one stone.

_____ 7. Samuel anointed David to be king over Israel.

_____ 8. David became king at age 40 and ruled Israel for 30 years.

_____ 9. David brought music and singing into the Tabernacle worship.

_____ 10. David was a man after God's heart.

_____ 11. The Lord is your Shepherd.

_____ 12. Judgment and mercy will follow you all your life.

Memory Verse: Psalms 23:1-6 (Day #50).

Books of the Old & New Testament: Add to the 54 books already learned: 2 Timothy, Titus, Philemon, Hebrews, James, 1 Peter.

Week 11

Families Working For God

Mordecai and Esther

Day #51   Moses, Aaron and Miriam

For I brought thee up out of the land of Egypt, and redeemed thee
out of the house of servants; and I sent before thee
Moses, Aaron, and Miriam.
Micah 6:4

Aaron, the son of Amram and Jochebed, was three years older than his brother, Moses. He also had an older sister named Miriam. They lived in Egypt where the evil Pharaoh had made slaves of all the Israelites living there. When all three children were grown, God used that family to deliver several million Jews from slavery in Egypt. God called Moses to be the leader of Israel, and Aaron was his helper. Together, Moses and Aaron appeared before Pharaoh on ten occasions to demand that he release the Israelites. Because Pharaoh refused every time, God sent ten plagues on the nation of Egypt. After the final plague, which brought death to the firstborn in every family, Pharaoh demanded that the Israelites get out of Egypt.

Later, the Tabernacle was built in the wilderness, and Aaron and his sons became priests. Other Levite relatives became the spiritual leaders of the Israelites. Moses and Aaron's sister, Miriam, played a part in saving baby Moses' life when she arranged with the Egyptian princess to have her own mother nurse Moses during his early years. Later, after the Israelites fled Egypt, she also used her tambourine to lead the people in songs of praise to God for delivering them from Egypt. Families who live for the Lord can be used greatly in God's Kingdom.

Prayer: *Lord Jesus, thank you for my family. Help us to serve you well and work together in your Kingdom. Amen.*

Day #52   **David and Solomon**

I have no greater joy than to hear that my children walk in truth.
3 John 1:4

Although David had many sons and daughters, God selected Solomon to be the son who would rule Israel after David. Because the prophet had told David this when Solomon was born, David trained Solomon his whole life to be a wise and Godly king. David had a desire to build a beautiful temple to worship God in, but God said that Solomon would build it instead. David saved money and treasures for the building of the Temple while he was alive. He taught Solomon how to be a wholehearted worshiper. Solomon was crowned king before David died, and David blessed God for allowing him to see his son reign over Israel.[33] For many years, Solomon followed David's teaching. He prayed to God for wisdom to lead the people, and God granted his request. He built the beautiful Temple and prayed powerful prayers, and even offered many sacrifices to God. Solomon recorded much of the wisdom that God gave him in the books of Proverbs and Ecclesiastes. If David could have lived to see the Temple and the reputation Solomon had around the world because of his wisdom, he would have been so happy. Children who grow up and follow the teachings of their parents make them very happy. Families who serve God together can see great things accomplished for His Kingdom.

Prayer: *Lord Jesus, I want to follow the Godly teachings of my parents so that we can do great things together for your Kingdom. Amen.*

Day #53   Mordecai and Esther

> *[Mordecai asked Esther] ...who knoweth whether thou art come to the kingdom for such a time as this?*
> Esther 4:14

Esther was a Jewish orphan who had grown up in Babylon. After her parents died, she was adopted by her cousin Mordecai who raised her as his own daughter, and she always obeyed everything he asked her to do. King Ahasuerus of Shushan banished Queen Vashti from the palace for disobeying a royal order, so he decided to find a new queen among the young ladies in his kingdom. Esther was very beautiful, and she was taken along with many other young ladies to the palace. When it finally came time for Esther to appear before the king, he chose her out of all the others he had seen. He placed the crown on her head and threw a huge party to celebrate finding a new queen. King Ahasuerus had a friend named Haman who had a strong dislike for Esther's cousin, Mordecai because Mordecai refused to bow when Haman walked by him. Because of this

---

[33] 1 Kings 1:48

disrespect, Haman received permission from the king to execute not only Mordecai, but also all the Jews in the kingdom. He didn't realize that Queen Esther was a Jew because she had not revealed her nationality. Mordecai sent a message to Esther asking her to speak to the king and save her people from death. She was very fearful at first, but he told her that perhaps God had allowed her to become queen just so she could save her people. After three days of prayer and fasting by all the Jews in Shushan, Esther appeared before the king and invited him and Haman to dinner. On the second night, Esther told the king about Haman's evil plan to kill all the Jews, and the angry king immediately had Haman executed. Mordecai was given Haman's position because Esther had told the king that he was her cousin. Esther's brave act saved her people.[34]

You never know when you may be placed in a position for a special purpose that only you can fulfill. If you will respect and obey your parents and other authorities in your life in the way that Esther obeyed Mordecai, then you will be ready to fulfill that special plan that God has for you and nobody else.

Prayer: *Lord Jesus, help me to be respectful and obedient to those who are my leaders so that when I am chosen for a special job, I will have the skills I need to do it well. Amen.*

Day #54   John Mark, Mary and Barnabas

And Barnabas and Saul returned from Jerusalem, when they had fulfilled their ministry, and took with them John, whose surname was Mark.
Acts 12:25

John Mark was a young man during the early days of the Church in Jerusalem. His mother, Mary, had a large home that was used for prayer meetings and other church gatherings. We don't know anything about Mark's dad, so it is assumed that his mother was a widow. Mark's uncle, Barnabas, was a preacher who sold his land and gave the money to the Church,[35] then he went on some missionary journeys with Paul. Mark was invited to go to Cyprus with Barnabas and Paul. He came home early, but

---

[34] Read the entire book of Esther to learn more about this fascinating story.
[35] Acts 4:36-37

later became a trusted assistant to Paul when Paul was in prison. Mark also was closely associated with Peter, and it is commonly thought that Peter told Mark the stories about Jesus that were written in the Gospel of Mark. Mark was greatly influenced by his mother and uncle, as well as other ministers in the early Church, and people are still being blessed by his example and writings today.

Prayer: *Lord Jesus, let me be willing to learn from great Christians in my family and in my Church so that I too can do great things for you that will affect others long after my life is finished. Amen.*

Day #55 Aquila and Priscilla

> *Greet Priscilla and Aquila my helpers in Christ Jesus:*
> *Likewise greet the church that is in their house…*
> Romans 16:3, 5[36]

Aquila and Priscilla were living in Corinth when they first met Paul. They had a tent-making business, and Paul, who was also a tent-maker, worked with them during the year and a half that he preached there. When Paul left Corinth to go to Ephesus, Aquila and Priscilla went with him. They opened their home for prayer and Church services. They witnessed to a preacher named Apollos and taught him some things about the Gospel that he didn't already know. They were lifetime friends and prayer partners with Paul. Husband and wife teams can be a powerful influence in their church and community. When you grow up and look for a husband or wife, make sure they are completely in love with God.

Prayer: *Lord Jesus, I know I'm too young right now to be thinking about finding a life-long mate, but I thank you for the Godly marriages that have influenced me in my walk with you, and I ask you to prepare the exact one you want me to have so that we too can be a Godly team to work together in your Kingdom until you come. Amen.*

---

[36] Other references to Aquila and Priscilla: Acts 18; 1 Corinthians 16:19; 2 Timothy 4:19.

Week 11 Review

Unscramble the names of the family members discussed in this week's lessons.

1. somes   _____
2. yarm   _____
3. ramma   _____
4, theres   _____
5, chedejob   _____
6. slonomo   _____
7. ulaiqa   _____
8. arano   _____
9. sanabbra   _____
10. cordimae   _____
11. vidad   _____
12. scilplair   _____
13. raimmi   _____
14. karm   _____

Memory Verse: 3 John 1:4 (Day #52).

Books of the Old & New Testament: Add to the 60 books already learned: 2 Peter, 1 John, 2 John, 3 John, Jude, Revelation.

Congratulations on learning all 66 books of the Bible.
It's time to celebrate!

Week 12

Jesus Loves Children

Day #56 Jesus Blesses Children

And they brought young children to him, that he should touch them: and his disciples rebuked those that brought them. But when Jesus saw it, he was much displeased, and said…, Suffer the little children to come unto me, and forbid them not: for of such is the kingdom of God. Verily I say unto you, Whosoever shall not receive the kingdom of God as a little child, he shall not enter therein. And he took them up in his arms, put his hands upon them, and blessed them.
Mark 10:13-16

One day Jesus was teaching some very important lessons about the family when people started bringing their children to Him so He could touch and bless them. Some of the grownups in the crowd didn't want little children to be bothering Jesus, so they tried to move them away from Him. But Jesus loves all the children, and He kindly stretched His arms out to the children. He told the grownups to let them come to Him because His Kingdom had room for everyone, especially children. Then Jesus hugged every child who came to Him, and He gave them a blessing.[37]

Prayer: *Lord Jesus, I wish I had lived during the time you were on earth so I could have been one of the children to get a hug and a blessing from you. Even though I can't see you, I have felt your presence when I was praying, reading your Word, or worshiping in a Church service. I am so happy that you love children and have included us in your plans to build your Church on earth. I love you Jesus. Amen.*

Day #57 Who Is The Greatest?

And [Jesus] asked them, What was it that ye disputed among yourselves by the way? But they held their peace: for by the way they had disputed among themselves, who should be the greatest. And he sat down, and called the twelve, and saith unto them, If any man desire to be first, the same shall be last of all, and servant of all. And he took a child, and set him in the midst of them: and when he had taken him in his arms, he said unto them, Whosoever shall receive one of such children in my name, receiveth me: and whosoever shall receive me, receiveth not me, but him that sent me.
Mark 9:33-37

---

[37] Matthew 19:13-15; Luke 18:15-17

Have you ever participated in a race to see who was the fastest? Maybe you entered a spelling bee to see who could spell the most words correctly. Perhaps you enjoy playing games like *Sorry* or *Monopoly* or *Scrabble* to see how often you can win. Competition is a part of life, and most people enjoy winning. In this story, the disciples had gotten into an argument about which one of them was the greatest. Even though Jesus didn't hear the argument, He knows everything you say or think. So, He brought a little child into the room and put it on His lap. He told His disciples that those who think they are in first place, are really in last place. Children also have a place in the Kingdom, and they should be received in Jesus' name.

Prayer: *Lord Jesus, I enjoy competing with others and winning. Help me to remember that the real winners in your Kingdom are those who are willing to serve others. Amen.*

Day #58   To Enter the Kingdom, Become As A Child

And Jesus called a little child unto him, and set him in the midst of them, And said, Verily I say unto you, Except ye be converted, and become as little children, ye shall not enter into the kingdom of heaven.
Matthew 18:2-3

Jesus is serious about the kind of attitude that He allows into Heaven. He told His disciples that their conversion experience needed to include becoming like a little child. Young children look up to adults and believe the things they say. They don't hold grudges; they argue, but make up quickly. As you grow up and become an adult, be careful to keep the childlike qualities of respect, faith, and forgiveness that Jesus loves.

Prayer: *Lord Jesus, your love for children is a comfort to me. Help me never lose those childlike qualities that make children so dear to your heart. I love you. Amen.*

Day #59   Don't Offend Children

And whoso shall receive one such little child in my name receiveth me. But whoso shall offend one of these little ones which believe in me, it were better for him that a millstone were hanged about his neck, and that he were drowned in the depth of the sea.
Matthew 18:5-6

Jesus loves children and is especially drawn to their natural faith, trust, obedience, respect and forgiveness. They have a special place in His Kingdom, and Jesus gives a strong rebuke to anyone who would dare offend a child and cause them to lose their faith. One time some religious leaders complained to Jesus that the children who were crying out praises to Jesus were making too much noise. They wanted Jesus to make them be quiet, but Jesus loves the praises of children, and He quoted an Old Testament scripture that says children's praise has the ability to silence the enemy.[38] So children, keep praising God, and don't be offended if some adults would rather that you kept quiet.

Prayer: *Lord Jesus, your Word tells me to make a joyful noise to you, clap my hands, and shout with a voice of triumph.[39] Help me to give you my best praise every time I go to your house to worship. Amen.*

Day #60 Be A Peacemaker

Blessed are the peacemakers: for they shall be called the children of God.
Matthew 5:9

One of the traits of God's children is that they try to keep peace rather than stirring up trouble. The Psalmist said to run away from evil and chase after peace. The New Testament writer, James, said that you sow the fruit of righteousness every time you make peace instead of fighting.[40] Make God happy by walking away from a fight, or speaking words of peace to end it.

Prayer: *Lord Jesus, I am your child. Search my heart for any seeds of hatred or troublemaking. Please remove them and replace them with seeds of peace and kindness. Amen.*

---

[38] Matthew 21:15-16; Psalms 8:2.
[39] Psalms 47:1; 66:1; 81:1; 95:1-2; 98:4-6; 100:1.
[40] Psalms 34:14; James 3:18.

Week 12 Review

Complete the crossword below

Across
2. Paul wrote 2 letters to him.
5. Answers for God's Word give people ____.
6. Give this when you are asked a question.
9. Timothy studied holy scriptures as a little ____.
10. Tempted Jesus 3 times.

Down
1. Words of ____ are found in the Bible.
3. How to hide Word in your heart
4. Devil told Jesus, Turn stones into this.
7. Do this so you won't be ashamed.
8. Hide God's Word in heart; don't ____ against God.

Memory Verse: Matthew 5:9 (Day #60).

Learn the names of the 12 sons of Jacob in alphabetical order in two weeks: Asher, Benjamin, Dan, Gad, Issachar, Joseph.

Week 13

New Testament Heroes

Day #61 Mary, Mother of Jesus

And the angel said unto her, Fear not, Mary: for thou hast found favour with God. And, behold, thou shalt...bring forth a son, and shalt call his name JESUS.
Luke 1:30-31

Mary was probably a young teenage girl when she was chosen to be the mother of Jesus. We are first introduced to her in the Bible when the angel Gabriel appeared to her and announced that she would become the mother of the Christ child. We know that she was engaged to be married to Joseph who was a carpenter, and we know that her pure and Godly lifestyle had brought her into favor with the Lord. We also know that she was good at keeping secrets, because many things that she didn't understand, she kept in her heart rather than talking about them.[41] Mary prompted Him to perform His first miracle at the wedding in Cana.[42] She followed Him and heard His teaching to the crowds.[43] She was at the cross when He died,[44] and was one of the 120 who followed Jesus' instructions to go back to Jerusalem and wait for the Holy Ghost. Throughout her life, she was a believer in Jesus, and even though she was His mother, she obeyed His teachings after He began His public ministry. She even became one of the first members of the New Testament church on the Day of Pentecost.[45]

Would you like to be a special child who finds favor with God? Jesus gave some instructions to help you find favor with Him. Here are just a few:

1) Become born again by being baptized in Jesus' name and being filled with God's Spirit.[46]
2) Love God and others with all your heart.[47]
3) Study His Word so you can obey all His commandments.[48]

---

[41] Luke 2:19, 51.
[42] John 2:1-11
[43] Luke 8:19-21
[44] John 19:25
[45] Acts 1:4-14
[46] John 3:1-8; Acts 2:37-39.
[47] Matthew 22:36-40
[48] John 14:15-21

Prayer: *Lord Jesus, Mary must have been a special lady to be chosen as your mother. Help me to follow you as faithfully as she did so that I too can find favor with you. Amen.*

Day #62 12-Year-Old Jesus

And Jesus increased in wisdom and stature, and in favour with God and man.
Luke 2:52

Joseph and Mary took their family to Jerusalem each year to celebrate the Passover. When Jesus was twelve years old, He went with His family and other friends to Jerusalem for the Passover. After the celebrations ended, all the travelers packed their things and headed back home, but Jesus decided to stay in Jerusalem without telling his mother and Joseph. After traveling a whole day, Mary realized that Jesus wasn't with anyone in their group, so she and Joseph returned to Jerusalem and spent three days looking for Him. They found Him in the Temple where He was discussing the scriptures with the doctors and religious leaders. The teachers were amazed at the scripture knowledge of one so young. When Mary scolded Jesus for staying behind without asking them, Jesus asked her why she didn't realize that He needed to be taking care of His Father's business. He meant His heavenly Father, but Mary and Joseph didn't understand at the time. Jesus returned home with them and obeyed their family rules until He became old enough to leave the house and begin His public ministry.[49]

Jesus was God wrapped in a human body, but He willingly submitted to the house rules and obeyed His mother and step-father as long as He lived in the home. If Jesus was willing to obey the house rules, how much more should you be willing to obey your parents without complaining?

Prayer: *Lord Jesus, even though you are God, you showed children everywhere how to honor and obey their parents even when the parents don't understand why their children do what they do. Help me to obey without talking back or showing a bad attitude. Amen.*

---

[49] For further study, read all of Luke 2.

Day #63   The Boy Who Shared His Lunch

*Every man according as he purposeth in his heart, so let him give;
not grudgingly, or of necessity: for God loveth a cheerful giver.*
2 Corinthians 9:7

One day while Jesus was teaching, He realized that the people were hungry, and He asked His disciples how they were going to feed them. Andrew answered that he had found a little boy with five barley loaves and two fishes, but he knew that would not be enough to feed the five thousand men plus women and children who were listening to Jesus' teaching. Jesus told Andrew it was enough, and He gave thanks for it, then began breaking it up and giving it to the disciples to pass out to the hungry people. The food kept growing as long as Jesus kept breaking it and passing it out. Finally everyone had eaten as much as they wanted, and there were twelve baskets of food left over![50]

We don't even know the name of the little boy who gave his lunch to Andrew to share with the crowd, but he learned that God loves those who cheerfully share what they have with others. It is very possible that he was able to take some of the leftovers home to share with his family.

Prayer: *Lord Jesus, help me to notice when other people need something that I have, and help me to cheerfully share what I have with them so they can be blessed for receiving, and I can be blessed for giving. Amen.*

Day #64   Rhoda

And as Peter knocked at the door of the gate, a damsel came to hearken, named Rhoda. And when she knew Peter's voice, she opened not the gate for gladness, but ran in, and told how Peter stood before the gate.
Acts 12:13-14

Peter was the most well-known leader in the Early Church. The evil King Herod wanted to kill him, so he had him arrested and put in prison. He intended to kill him right after the Passover celebration. The Church leaders called a prayer meeting at Mary's home. One of Mary's maids was

---

[50] John 6:5-14

a young girl named Rhoda. While the Church people were praying for Peter's release, an angel went into the prison and removed Peter's chains and led him right past the guards and through the locked prison gate. Then Peter hurried to Mary's house where prayer was taking place. The young Rhoda had the privilege of being the one to answer Peter's knock. No doubt she had heard him preach many times, and she knew his voice. Her excitement made her forget to open the door; instead, she ran into the room where the people were praying and excitedly announced that Peter was at the door. They laughed and made fun of her, but she insisted until they all went to the door and opened it to find Peter standing there. He came in and explained how an angel had delivered him.[51]

While Rhoda was busy serving and answering the door, she was able to be the first one to witness a miraculous answer to prayer. You may feel like the little jobs you are asked to do in the Church are not very important, but do them to the best of your ability, for you never know when God may choose you to be the first witness of a miracle.

Prayer: *Lord Jesus, I believe in the power of prayer. If I get tired of going to prayer meetings with my parents or helping with little jobs around the church, help me to remember Rhoda. I don't want to miss out on seeing a miracle. Amen.*

Day #65   Timothy

To Timothy, my dearly beloved son: Grace, mercy, and peace, from God the Father and Christ Jesus our Lord. I thank God, whom I serve from my forefathers with pure conscience, that without ceasing I have remembrance of thee in my prayers night and day; Greatly desiring to see thee, being mindful of thy tears, that I may be filled with joy; When I call to remembrance the unfeigned faith that is in thee, which dwelt first in thy grandmother Lois, and thy mother Eunice; and I am persuaded that in thee also.
2 Timothy 1:2-5

Timothy's dad was an unbeliever,[52] but his mother, Eunice, and his grandmother, Lois, made sure that he was taught the basic truths of Christian living. As he grew into a young man, Paul took an interest in him

---

[51] To read the whole story, read Acts 12.
[52] Acts 16:1

and became a Godly role-model for him. Paul even took him on missionary journeys with him. He called Timothy his son in the faith.[53] Later, God called Timothy to be a preacher, and Paul sometimes sent Timothy to preach in Churches where he could not go himself.

If one or both of your parents are unbelievers, find a Godly role-model who can be an example of a Christian man or woman and follow their example. God can use you in a great way if you have the genuine faith that Paul saw in Timothy and his mother and grandmother.

Prayer: *Lord Jesus, I want to live my life so that others will see my genuine faith in you, and they will want to know Jesus like I do. Amen.*

---

[53] Son in the faith – 1 Cor. 4:17; Phil. 2:19-22; 1 Tim. 1:2, 18; 2 Tim. 1:2

Week 13 Review

Match the definitions on the left to the words on the right.

1. Mother of Jesus   ___ Eunice

2. Jesus' first miracle performed here.   ___ Temple

3. The angel who gave the message about Jesus.   ___ Angel

4. Joseph and Mary went to Jerusalem for ____.   ___ Cana

5. Place Jesus talked with religious leaders.   ___ Herod

6. Amount of bread and fish that fed over 5,000.   ___ Mary

7. Disciple who brought the boy's lunch to Jesus.   ___ Paul

8. Evil king who arrested Peter.   ___ Andrew

9. Mary's servant girl.   ___ Lois

10. Who rescued Peter from prison?   ___ Gabriel

11. Timothy's mother.   ___ Rhoda

12. Timothy's grandmother.   ___ 5 and 2

13. He called Timothy his son in the faith.   ___ Passover

Memory Verse: 2 Corinthians 9:7 (Day #63).

Learn the names of the 12 sons of Jacob in alphabetical order in two weeks: Judah, Levi, Naphtali, Reuben, Simeon, Zebulun.

Congratulations on learning all 12 of the sons of Jacob.
It's time to celebrate!

Week 14

There Is Only One God

For unto us a child is born, unto us a son is given: and the government shall be upon his shoulder: and his name shall be called Wonderful, Counsellor, The mighty God, The everlasting Father, The Prince of Peace.
Isaiah 9:6

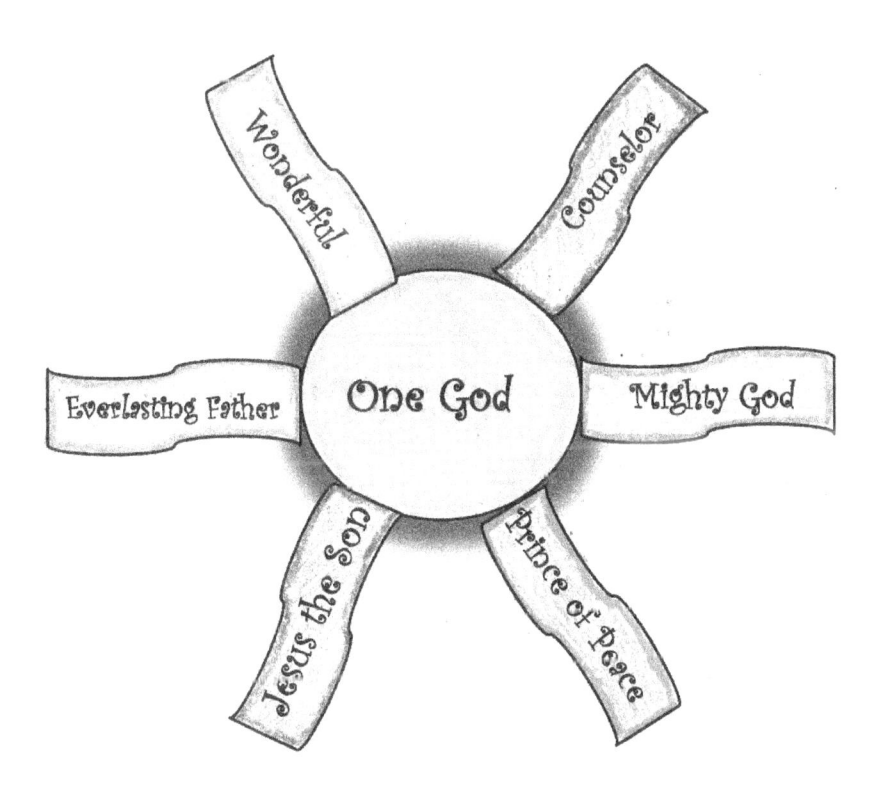

Day #66   Love God Wholeheartedly

Hear, O Israel: The LORD our God is one LORD: And thou shalt love the LORD thy God with all thine heart, and with all thy soul, and with all thy might.
Deuteronomy 6:4-5

When Moses gave this law to the Israelites, they were on their way to establishing new homes in Canaan, the land of promise. Because the people in Canaan worshiped many gods, Moses wanted to make sure that the Israelites would not be influenced by the worship of their new neighbors. Today, many people give their worship to false gods instead of the one true God. Some people worship gods named Allah and Buddha. But other things, like entertainment, books you read, or games you play can become gods to you if they take away your time from loving God, and studying His Word to learn more about Him and His laws. Make sure that the one true God always has first place in your heart and actions.

Prayer: *Lord Jesus, I am thankful that I know who you are, and I want to love you with my whole heart, soul, and might. Amen.*

Day #67   One God Who Is Everywhere

One Lord, one faith, one baptism, One God and Father of all, who is above all, and through all, and in you all.
Ephesians 4:5-6

The people of the ancient city of Ephesus worshiped a false goddess named Diana. Silversmiths made lots of money by making silver idols of the goddess. When Paul came to town and preached that there was only one God whose name was Jesus Christ, the silversmiths started a riot because they were afraid they would go out of business if people quit buying the silver idols they made.[54] Paul preached for two years in Ephesus and raised up a strong one-God Church in that city.

Prayer: *Lord Jesus, I am thankful that I know that you are the only true God and that you are greater than any other power in this world. Amen.*

---

[54] Acts 19:23-41.

Day #68   God Became Flesh

*In the beginning was the Word, and the Word was with God, and **the Word was God**. And the Word [**God**] was made flesh, and dwelt among us, (and we beheld his glory, the glory as of the only begotten of the Father,) full of grace and truth.*
John 1:1, 14[55]

In Genesis chapter 1, God spoke the heavens and the earth into existence. He then spoke everything on earth into existence. John said in chapter one of his gospel that the Word was God. Then he taught in verse 14 of chapter one that God became flesh and lived on the earth so that people could see God's glory shining from the man, Christ Jesus. One God, who was an invisible Spirit, made a body for Himself, and put His Spirit into that body so that people could finally see what God looked like. Jesus later made the statement, *"I and my Father are one."*[56] One Spirit in One body = One God!

Prayer: *Lord Jesus, thank you for your powerful Word that spoke everything we see into existence. It is exciting to know that you are the mighty God who came to earth in a body so that people could see you. Amen.*

Day #69   When You See Jesus, You Have Seen The Father

Jesus saith unto him, Have I been so long time with you, and yet hast thou not known me, Philip? he that hath seen me hath seen the Father; and how sayest thou then, Show us the Father? Believest thou not that I am in the Father, and the Father in me? the words that I speak unto you I speak not of myself: but the Father that dwelleth in me, he doeth the works.
John 14:9-10

One day Jesus told His disciples that He would soon be going away to prepare a place where they would be able to come and live with Him forever. He stated that He was the way, the truth and the life. Philip then asked Jesus to show them the Father. Jesus' reply was eye-opening to Philip and the other disciples. *When you see Jesus, you have seen the Father.*[57] Because the Father is invisible, the visible body of Jesus is the only way

---

[55] For further study on this subject, see this scripture: Acts 20:28.
[56] John 10:30.
[57] John 14.

your eyes can see the Father. The Old Testament prophet Isaiah said that the child who would be born, would be called *the mighty God and the everlasting Father*. He even said that the child would be called *Immanuel,* which meant *God with us*.[58] One God in One Body = Jesus.

Prayer: *Lord Jesus, thank you for coming to earth to die for my sins. I wish I could've seen the look on Philip's face the night you told him that when he looked at you, he was looking at the Father. Thank you for letting John write about this occasion so that we too could understand who you really are. In Jesus' name. Amen.*

Day #70   The One True God Is Your Redeemer

> *Thus saith the LORD, thy Redeemer, the Holy One of Israel;*
> *I am the LORD thy God which teacheth thee to profit,*
> *which leadeth thee by the way that thou shouldest go.*
> Isaiah 48:17

When Adam and Eve were first created, they were holy and without sin, but after they sinned in the Garden of Eden, the devil claimed the right to their souls. From that day forward, every person born into this world was born with a sinful nature, and the devil has worked very hard to persuade people to love him instead of God. The good news is that the one true God is your Redeemer. That means that He paid the price with His blood on the cross to buy back His people from the devil. Although the price for your salvation has been paid, you have to take steps to obey God's plan to receive your own personal salvation experience.[59] Follow His Word and His ministers of the Gospel to learn more about how to live a successful Christian life.

Prayer: *Lord Jesus, thank you for your death on the cross that paid for my sins. You are holy, and I want to learn more about you every day so that I too can be holy like you. Amen.*

---

[58] Isaiah 9:6; 7:14; Matthew 1:21-23.
[59] For more information on how to be Born Again, see the devotions in Weeks 15 and 16.

The God of the Old Testament is the same Jesus of the New Testament.[60]

WHEEL OF PROPHECY
WHO IS GOD?

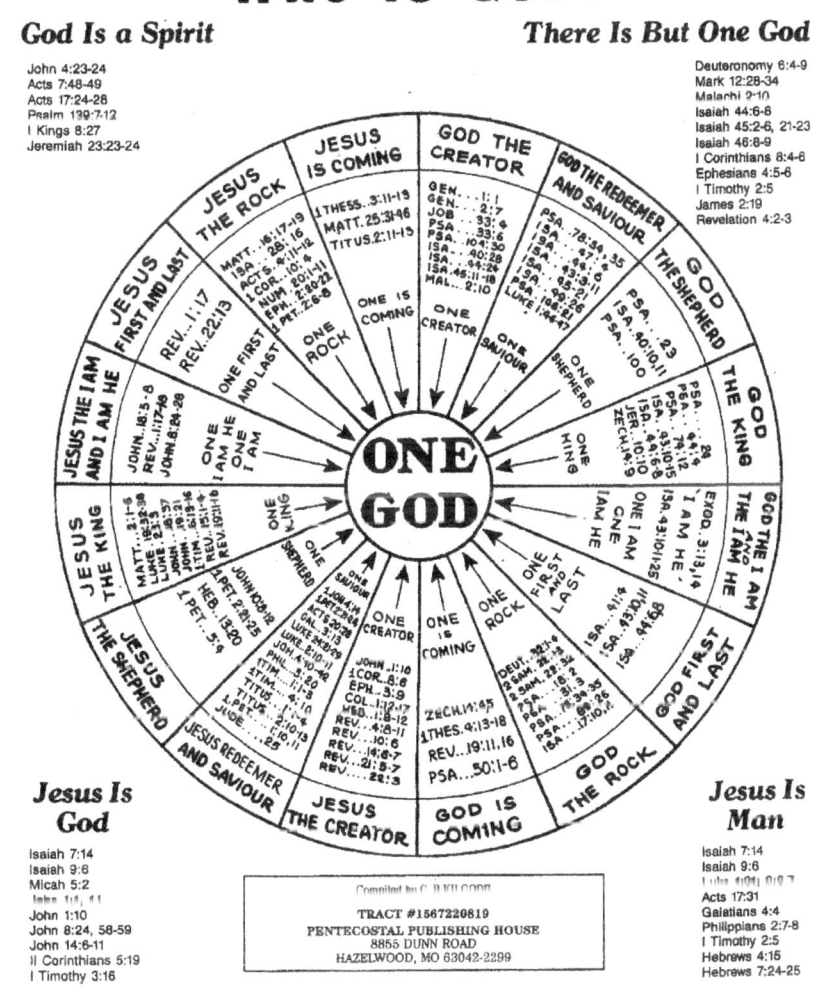

God Is a Spirit

John 4:23-24
Acts 7:48-49
Acts 17:24-28
Psalm 139:7-12
I Kings 8:27
Jeremiah 23:23-24

There Is But One God

Deuteronomy 6:4-9
Mark 12:28-34
Malachi 2:10
Isaiah 44:6-8
Isaiah 45:2-6, 21-23
Isaiah 46:8-9
I Corinthians 8:4-6
Ephesians 4:5-6
I Timothy 2:5
James 2:19
Revelation 4:2-3

Jesus Is God

Isaiah 7:14
Isaiah 9:6
Micah 5:2
John 1:1, 14
John 1:10
John 8:24, 58-59
John 14:6-11
II Corinthians 5:19
I Timothy 3:16

TRACT #1567220819
PENTECOSTAL PUBLISHING HOUSE
8855 DUNN ROAD
HAZELWOOD, MO 63042-2299

Jesus Is Man

Isaiah 7:14
Isaiah 9:6
Luke 1:31; 2:1-7
Acts 17:31
Galatians 4:4
Philippians 2:7-8
I Timothy 2:5
Hebrews 4:15
Hebrews 7:24-25

---

[60] Wheel of Prophecy used by permission from the Pentecostal Publishing House. This tract can be purchased from pentecostalpublishing.com.

Week 14 Review

Fill in the blanks in the sentences below.

Hear, O _____: The LORD our God is _____ LORD: And thou shalt love the LORD thy God with all thine _____, and with all thy _____, and with all thy _____. One _____, one _____, one _____, One ____ and _____ of all, who is _____ all, and _____ all, and ____ you all. In the beginning was the _____, and the Word was with God, and the Word _____ God. And the Word [**God**] was _____ _____, and dwelt among us, (and we _____ his glory, the glory as of the only begotten of the Father,) full of _____ and _____. I and my _____ are _____. Jesus saith unto him, Have I been so long time with you, and yet hast thou not _____ ____, Philip? he that hath seen ____ hath seen the _____; and how sayest thou then, Show us the Father? Believest thou not that I am ____ the Father, and the Father ____ me? the words that I speak unto you I speak not of _____: but the _____ that dwelleth ____ me, he doeth the works.

Memory Verse: Isaiah 9:6 - *For unto us a child is born, unto us a son is given: and the government shall be upon his shoulder: and his name shall be called Wonderful, Counsellor,* **The mighty God, The everlasting Father***, The Prince of Peace.*

Learn the names of the 12 disciples in two weeks: Peter & Andrew (brothers) James & John (brothers, sons of Zebedee), Philip, Bartholomew. (Matthew 10:2-4; Mark 3:16-19; Luke 6:13-16).

Week 15

You Must Be Born Again

The Day of Pentecost

Day #71   Jesus Teaches the New Birth

Jesus answered and said unto him, Verily, verily, I say unto thee,
Except a man be born again, he cannot see the kingdom of God.
Jesus answered, Verily, verily, I say unto thee,
Except a man be born of water and of the Spirit,
he cannot enter into the kingdom of God.
John 3:3, 5

In a conversation with an important religious leader named Nicodemus, Jesus taught him that if He wanted to *see* God's Kingdom, he had to be born again. Then Jesus explained more specifically that the way to be born again was to be baptized and be filled with God's Spirit. He said if Nicodemus obeyed these two instructions, he would be allowed to enter God's Kingdom. Do you want to become a part of God's family? Then the steps of water baptism and receiving God's Spirit are what Jesus said we must do.

Prayer: *Lord Jesus, I don't only want to watch other people enjoy being Christians. I want to become one myself. Guide me through the step of baptism, and fill me with your Spirit so that I too can enjoy the benefits of being your child.*

Day #72   The Great Commission

*And that repentance and remission of sins should be preached **in his name***
among all nations, beginning at Jerusalem. And, behold, I send
the promise of my Father upon you: but tarry ye in the city of Jerusalem,
until ye be endued with power from on high.
Luke 24:47, 49

Before Jesus went back to Heaven, He gave His disciples instructions for going out and preaching the Gospel around the world. These last instructions are often called the *Great Commission*. These instructions can be found in all four of the Gospels (Matthew, Mark, Luke, and John) and in the first chapter of the book of Acts.[61] When you combine what Jesus said in all five of these passages of scripture, you can understand what Jesus

---

[61] Matthew 28:18-20; Mark 16:15-20; Luke 24:46-53; John 20:21-23; Acts 1:1-14.

wanted the disciples to teach everyone in the world. Here is a list containing all the parts of the *Great Commission*:

1. Belief in Jesus

2. Repentance

3. Water baptism in Jesus' name

4. Be filled with the Holy Ghost

5. Teach others

6. Healings and miracles

Prayer: *Lord Jesus, when I have obeyed the first four parts of the Great Commission, help me to share my experience with others, and let the signs of a believer follow my life so that others can see that you are living in me. Amen.*

Day #73   What is the Gospel?

Moreover, brethren, I declare unto you the gospel which I preached unto you, which also ye have received, and wherein ye stand; By which also ye are saved, if ye keep in memory what I preached unto you, unless ye have believed in vain. For I delivered unto you first of all that which I also received, how that Christ died for our sins according to the scriptures; And that he was buried, and that he rose again the third day according to the scriptures:
1 Corinthians 15:1-4

After Jesus rose from the dead, He gave some instructions to His disciples before He went back to Heaven. One of the last things He told them was to go into all the world and preach the Gospel to every creature.[62] Several years later, Paul wrote to the Corinthian church and said that he had preached the Gospel to them, and they would be saved if they obeyed the three parts of the Gospel which are the death, burial, and resurrection of Jesus.

How can you obey Jesus' death, burial and resurrection? On the Day of Pentecost, Peter said that you must repent of your sins, be baptized in

---

[62] Mark 16:15.

Jesus' name to wash away your sins, and be filled with the Holy Ghost.[63] If you take these three steps, you will have obeyed the Gospel.

Prayer: *Lord Jesus, by faith I want to obey the Gospel that will save my soul by repenting of my sins, getting baptized in your name, and letting you fill me with your Holy Spirit. Amen.*

Day #74   Peter Teaches Salvation to the Jews

Now when they heard this, they were pricked in their heart, and said unto Peter and to the rest of the apostles, Men and brethren, what shall we do? Then Peter said unto them, Repent, and be baptized every one of you in the name of Jesus Christ for the remission of sins, and ye shall receive the gift of the Holy Ghost.
Acts 2:37-38

The very first man and woman God created disobeyed one of God's rules, and their sinfulness was passed on to every person who has been born since then. Jesus came into the world to die for our sins, and once His mission was accomplished, He told His disciples to teach others what they needed to do to be saved. Peter preached the very first salvation sermon in Acts chapter 2. When people asked the question, "What shall we do?" Peter told them to repent of their sins.[64] Then He instructed them to be baptized in the name of their Savior, Jesus Christ, so their sins could be washed away. Finally, God promised to give them the gift of the Holy Ghost which means that Jesus would come to live inside of them. The people in the book of Acts always spoke in a language they had not learned when the Holy Ghost came into their heart.[65] Have you obeyed Acts 2:37-38? It is your ticket to becoming a member of God's family.

Prayer: *Lord Jesus, it is easy to do wrong things and hard to be good all the time. Forgive me for the wrong things I think and say and do. I want to be saved from my sins and tell others about the exciting changes you have made in my life. Amen.*

---

[63] Acts 2:37-39; Romans 6:3-5.
[64] Jesus taught repentance: Matthew 4:17; Mark 2:17; Luke 5:32; 13:3; 24:47.
[65] Jews-Acts 2:1-4; Samaritans-Acts 8:14-19; Gentiles-Acts 10:44-48; Believers-Acts 19:1-6

Day #75   Peter Teaches Salvation to the Gentiles

While Peter yet spake these words, the Holy Ghost fell on all them which heard the word. And they of the circumcision which believed were astonished, as many as came with Peter, because that on the Gentiles also was poured out the gift of the Holy Ghost. For they heard them speak with tongues, and magnify God. Then answered Peter, Can any man forbid water, that these should not be baptized, which have received the Holy Ghost as well as we?
And he commanded them to be baptized in the name of the Lord...
Acts 10:44-48

Acts 10 tells the story of a very good man who was a Gentile. That means he was not a Jew. Cornelius prayed all the time and gave lots of money to people who needed it, but he wasn't saved.[66] One day while he was praying, an angel appeared to him and told him to bring Peter to his house so Peter could tell him what he needed to do to be saved.[67] Peter and six other Jews came to Cornelius' house and preached the Gospel of Jesus' death, burial and resurrection to them. Right in the middle of Peter's sermon, God interrupted Peter by filling everyone with the Holy Ghost. The six Jews knew the Gentiles had received the Holy Ghost because they heard them speaking in tongues. So Peter told those Gentiles that since they had received the Holy Ghost exactly like the Jews had, they would have to be baptized the same way the Jews were, which was in the name of the Lord Jesus.

If you have been praying for salvation, the pattern for Jews and non-Jews is exactly the same. Repent, be baptized in water in Jesus' name, and receive the gift of the Holy Ghost, speaking in other tongues.

Prayer: *Lord Jesus, I'm thankful that the New Testament plan of salvation includes everyone, even young boys and girls. Amen.*

---

[66] Acts 11:13-14.
[67] Acts 10:1-6.

Week 15 Review

Unscramble the following words below. Baptism - Burial – Cornelius - Death - Gospel – HolyGhost - Jerusalem - Nicodemus – repentance - resurrection – salvation – tongues.

1. micunsode   _____

2. laserjume   _____

3. plegos   _____

4. hadet   _____

5. ribula   _____

6. norcustrerio   _____

7. vanostila   _____

8. tranceneep   _____

9. spatbim   _____

10. shotloghy   _____

11. snutego   _____

12. clerinuso   _____

Memory Verse: Acts 2:38 (Day #74)

Learn the names of the 12 disciples in two weeks: Thomas, Matthew, James (son of Alphaeus), Thaddaeus, Simon Zelotes, and Judas Iscariot. (Matthew 10:2-4; Mark 3:16-19; Luke 6:13-16).

Congratulations on learning all 12 of the disciples of Jesus.
It's time to celebrate!

Week 16

Basics For New Believers

Jesus' baptism

Day #76   Paul Teaches Salvation to Believers

...Paul...came to Ephesus: and finding certain disciples, He said unto them, Have ye received the Holy Ghost since ye believed? And they said unto him, We have not so much as heard whether there be any Holy Ghost. And he said unto them, Unto what then were ye baptized? And they said, Unto John's baptism. Then said Paul, John verily baptized with the baptism of repentance, saying unto the people, that they should believe on him which should come after him, that is, on Christ Jesus. When they heard this, they were baptized in the name of the Lord Jesus. And when Paul had laid his hands upon them, the Holy Ghost came on them; and they spake with tongues, and prophesied.
Acts 19:1-6

One day Paul was traveling through the city of Ephesus, and he met a group of twelve men who told him they were believers. Paul had two questions for them. He first asked if they had received the Holy Ghost since they became a believer. They had never heard of it. His second question concerned how they had been baptized. They said they were baptized according to John the Baptist's teaching. Paul told them that they needed to update their experience by getting rebaptized in Jesus' name. Consequently, they were baptized over again. Then Paul prayed for them, and they were all filled with the Holy Ghost and spoke in other tongues.

Many people today say they believe on the Lord Jesus Christ as their Savior, but if they haven't experienced Jesus' name baptism and receiving the Holy Ghost, this chapter reveals the pattern that Paul used to convince them that they should be rebaptized, and also receive the Holy Ghost.[68]

Prayer: *Lord Jesus, I am thankful for the pattern for salvation that you gave us in the book of Acts so we wouldn't make a mistake about what we need to do. Amen.*

---

[68] Jesus said that all believers should receive the Holy Ghost. (John 7:37-39).

Day #77   Baptism is Done by Immersion in Water

And Jesus, when he was baptized, went up straightway out of the water:
Matthew 3:16

Before Jesus began His public ministry, He found His cousin, John the Baptist, and asked John to baptize Him. John and Jesus both went down into the water, and Jesus was baptized by being totally immersed in the water. Every time someone was baptized in the Bible, they were always baptized by immersion.[69] Because the purpose of baptism is to wash away a person's sins after they have repented, a person must be old enough to understand that they are a sinner and ask for forgiveness for their sins. Since infants have no understanding of sin, the Apostles did not teach or practice the baptism of infants.

Prayer: *Lord Jesus, even though you never had any sins to repent of, I am thankful that you showed us the way to be baptized when you went down into the water with John the Baptist. Amen.*

Day #78   Understanding Matthew 28:19

Go ye therefore, and teach all nations, baptizing them in the name of the Father, and of the Son, and of the Holy Ghost:
Matthew 28:19

Jesus gave instructions for baptizing new believers in this passage of scripture. Sometimes people misunderstand what He meant, and instead of obeying His words, they simply repeat what He said. This verse said that baptism should be performed in the NAME of the Father, Son, and Holy Ghost. Those words are simply titles that explain some of the roles God fills. You are a son or daughter, or a brother or sister, but you also have a name. God has many titles such as the good *Shepherd*, the *Vine*, the *Light* of the world and many others, but He only has one name, and that name is Jesus. Jesus is the name of the Father, Son, and Holy Ghost.[70] That is why the disciples always baptized in the name of Jesus Christ,[71] for that

---

[69] Other examples of baptism by immersion: John 3:23; Acts 8:36-39.
[70] Father-John 5:43; Son-Matthew 1:21; John 20:30-31; Holy Ghost-John 14:26.
[71] Scripture support for Jesus name baptism: Luke 24:47; Acts 2:38; 8:16; 10:48; 19:3-5; 22:16; 1 Corinthians 6:11; Galatians 3:27.

name is the saving name[72] and the name by which the family of God is identified.

Prayer: *Lord Jesus, thank you for helping me to understand the importance of having your name applied to my life when I am baptized. Amen.*

Day #79   Confessing Sin After Conversion

If we say that we have no sin, we deceive ourselves, and the truth is not in us.
If we confess our sins, he is faithful and just to forgive us our sins,
and to cleanse us from all unrighteousness.
1 John 1:8-9

It is very easy to compare yourself with really bad people like Adolph Hitler, or the terrorists who flew their planes into the World Trade Center, and think that you are good by comparison. But you can't measure yourself with others. God's Word is the measuring stick to show you if you are right or wrong. What happens when you sin after you have been born again? Do you have to get baptized all over again every time you do something wrong? This verse shows you that you simply need to ask Jesus to forgive you, and He will wash your sin away, and you will be clean in His eyes, just as though you were baptized again.

Prayer: *Lord Jesus, even after I am born again, I will still have moments when I do something wrong. Thank you for the promise that if I confess my sins to you, you will forgive me and wash away all the sin in my heart. Amen.*

---

[72] Acts 4:12.

Day #80   Do Everything in Jesus' Name

And whatsoever ye do in word or deed,
do all in the name of the Lord Jesus,
giving thanks to God and the Father by him.
Colossians 3:17

One day Peter and John went to the Temple to pray. Before they went inside, they met a man who couldn't walk, and he was begging for people to give him some money. Peter boldly told him they didn't have money, but what they had was far more powerful. He then commanded in the name of Jesus for the man to stand up and walk. The man stood up and went into the Temple with them, walking and leaping and praising God all the way.[73] Jesus said that His followers would be able to heal people and perform miracles in His name. The very first miracle in the New Testament Church was performed in the name of Jesus. Paul said that everything we do should be done in Jesus' name. That means to pray, heal, preach, teach, comfort the hurting, and even baptize in Jesus' name, for there is power in that name.

Prayer: *Lord Jesus, your name is holy and powerful. Thank you for allowing us to use your name to perform miraculous works. I will be careful to always say your name reverently and not use it as a swear word or in a joking way. Amen.*

---

[73] Acts 3:1-10.

Week 16 Review

Find the following words in the grid below.

Baptize Believers Confess Ephesus Family Father Forgive Heal Holy HolyGhost Immersion Jesus John Miracle Name Paul Peter Power Powerful Repentance Salvation Son Temple Tongues Walk Water

R	D	X	L	U	A	P	C	R	E	M	A	N	Q	U	F	R
J	V	A	U	Y	C	O	N	F	E	S	S	R	N	A	Y	S
V	V	L	F	J	J	C	K	Y	S	T	T	Y	M	N	A	B
E	P	T	R	M	I	R	A	C	L	E	A	I	D	L	E	E
R	E	P	E	N	T	A	N	C	E	H	L	W	V	L	V	T
N	T	I	W	M	T	M	P	Q	N	Y	I	A	I	I	W	O
P	E	H	O	K	P	Y	R	F	Q	M	T	E	G	O	Y	N
W	R	R	P	W	P	L	F	E	G	I	V	R	E	X	N	G
R	E	H	T	A	F	S	E	B	O	E	O	B	M	N	O	U
E	P	H	E	S	U	S	U	N	R	F	L	C	V	E	I	E
E	H	O	L	Y	G	H	O	S	T	A	N	R	C	Z	S	S
H	E	S	N	H	O	J	E	F	E	C	W	E	J	I	R	L
C	O	E	N	I	M	Z	K	H	F	J	L	W	S	T	E	B
O	V	L	R	W	I	J	D	L	A	C	R	O	B	P	M	L
L	E	Y	Y	T	W	O	I	Y	A	E	N	P	B	A	M	E
Y	R	D	P	F	H	H	K	R	H	W	R	Y	L	B	I	A

Memory Verse: <u>Colossians 3:17</u> (Day #80)

Also memorize: <u>Acts 4:12</u> - *Neither is there salvation in any other: for there is none other name under heaven given among men, whereby we must be saved.*

Week 17

Love Covers All

1 John 4:8

Day #81   God Died For Your Sins

For God so loved the world, that he gave his only begotten Son, that whosoever believeth in him should not perish, but have everlasting life.
John 3:16

*Hereby perceive we the **love of God, because he laid down his life** for us: and we ought to lay down our lives for the brethren.*
1 John 3:16

The apostle John wrote in chapter 1 of his gospel that God became flesh and lived on earth.[74] With that in mind, we can conclude that because God, the invisible Spirit, loved the world so much, He created Himself a body and called that body His Son. He then put His Spirit inside that body, and He came to earth to die for your sins. God did not send a separate person to die for your sins. He came and laid down His life so you could be saved.

Prayer: *Lord Jesus, thank you for helping me understand that your love did not cause you to send someone else to die for me. You came yourself. Thank you for loving me that much. Amen.*

Day #82   The Two Greatest Commandments

Jesus said unto him, Thou shalt love the Lord thy God with all thy heart, and with all thy soul, and with all thy mind. This is the first and great commandment. And the second is like unto it, Thou shalt love thy neighbour as thyself. On these two commandments hang all the law and the prophets.
Matthew 22:37-40

In the Old Testament, Moses gave the Israelites Ten Commandments to live by. But when Jesus came, He rolled all the Ten Commandments into just two for people to obey. He said all the other commandments hung on loving God and loving each other. If I love God, I will gladly obey His laws. If I love others, I will not steal from them or lie about them. So if you have trouble remembering the Ten Commandments, just remember that people who love God and love others do not break His commandments.

---

[74] John 1:1, 14.

Prayer: *Lord Jesus, it will be easy for me to remember the top two commandments you told us to obey. It is not always easy to love others, especially when they hurt my feelings, but I will work really hard to love others like you love me. Amen.*

Day #83   A New Commandment

A new commandment I give unto you,
That ye love one another; as I have loved you, that ye also love one another.
By this shall all men know that ye are my disciples, if ye have love one to another.
John 13:34-35

Jesus had told His disciples that the two greatest commandments were to love God and love others, but on the night that He was arrested, He gave them a new commandment. This time He told them to love one another in the same way He loved them. He said that others would know they were His disciples if they had love for each other. Often people outside the Church are hurting, and they feel unloved. They look to the Church to see how the members treat each other. If they can see that everyone loves each other and takes care of each other's needs, they will know that this Church is the *real deal*. What do outsiders see when they look at the members of your church?

Prayer: *Lord Jesus, let me love the members in my local Church and pay attention to their needs so that unbelievers will be drawn to you, because we have the kind of love they are looking for. Amen.*

Day #84   Obedience Proves Your Love

If ye love me, keep my commandments. He that hath my commandments,
and keepeth them, he it is that loveth me: and he that loveth me
shall be loved of my Father, and I will love him, and will manifest myself to him.
John 14:15, 21

It is very easy to say you love Jesus, but He created a little test to help Him know if you are just saying words, or if you really do love Him. The proof of your love for Jesus is shown by how well you obey His rules. Of course, you must study His rule book, the Holy Bible, so you will know what rules you are supposed to obey. The good news is that Jesus loves those who obey His rules, and He lets those people get to know Him in a more special way than the ones who don't obey His rules.

Prayer: *Lord Jesus, I really do want to know you better. I am making an effort to learn more about your Word, so that I can be obedient to all of your rules. Thank you for your Word. Amen.*

Day #85   Love Your Enemies

*But I say unto you which hear, Love your enemies,
do good to them which hate you, Bless them that curse you,
and pray for them which despitefully use you.*
Luke 6:27-28

One day while Jesus was teaching, He spoke about loving your enemies and doing nice things for those who hate you. He even said to pray for those who do hateful things to you. When Jesus was hanging on the cross, He showed us how to forgive and pray for those who hate us. His enemies had beat Him and tortured Him until blood was running down His face and His back. Then they nailed Him to a cross to die. Even though He was in terrible pain from the beatings, Jesus prayed this prayer for His enemies: *"Father, forgive them; for they know not what they do."*[75]

Prayer: *Lord Jesus, I need your help with this verse. When people do mean things to me or my friends, I want to punch them and make them suffer for the mean things they have done. Help me learn how to forgive and pray for those who are hateful. Amen.*

---

[75] Luke 23:34.

Week 17 Review

Answer True or False for each statement below.

_____ 1. John said God became flesh and lived on earth.

_____ 2. God put His Spirit inside a body and called it the Holy Ghost.

_____ 3. Jesus said to love God halfheartedly.

_____ 4. The two great commandments are to love God and love others.

_____ 5. The world will know you are Jesus' disciple by the way you talk.

_____ 6. Jesus said to love others in the same way He loves you.

_____ 7. If you love God, you will obey only the rules that you like.

_____ 8. You prove your love to Jesus by obeying His commandments.

_____ 9. Jesus taught that you should love your enemies.

_____ 10. Jesus said to do nice things only for those who love you.

_____ 11. On the cross Jesus prayed for punishment for His enemies.

_____ 12. Jesus said to pray for those who do hateful things to you.

Memory Verse: John 3:16 and 1 John 3:16 (Day #81)

Also memorize: Romans 8:28 - *And we know that all things work together for good to them that love God, to them who are the called according to his purpose.*

Week 18

Prayer

RYDER age 5

"Now I lay me down to sleep"

Day #86   The Lord's Prayer

After this manner therefore pray ye: Our Father which art in heaven, Hallowed be thy name. Thy kingdom come, Thy will be done in earth, as it is in heaven. Give us this day our daily bread. And forgive us our debts, as we forgive our debtors. And lead us not into temptation, but deliver us from evil: For thine is the kingdom, and the power, and the glory, for ever. Amen.
Matthew 6:9-13

Jesus' disciples saw Him praying every day, and one day they asked Him if He would teach them to pray. The prayer that Jesus gave them has become the best known prayer in the Bible, and it is quoted in many Churches every service. This prayer teaches you that God is your Father, and His name is holy. It teaches you to pray for God's will in your decisions and to pray for your daily food provision. It teaches you to ask God to forgive your wrongs and for you to forgive the wrongs of others against you. It teaches you to ask for protection from evil and to acknowledge that God's Kingdom has all the power and glory forever. If you don't know this prayer, now would be a good time to memorize it.

Prayer: *Lord Jesus, thank you for giving me this prayer so I can learn how to pray more effectively. Amen.*

Day #87   Don't Worry! Pray!

Be careful for nothing; but in every thing by prayer and supplication with thanksgiving let your requests be made known unto God.
Philippians 4:6

Don't worry about anything. Take your problems to the Lord in prayer, and then give Him thanks for hearing your prayers.

Prayer: *Lord Jesus, sometimes I get stressed with all the homework and house chores that I am expected to do. I need you to calm my worries and give me peace. Thank you for listening and caring about me.*

Day #88 You Cannot Hide Sin From God

*I acknowledge my sin unto thee, and mine iniquity have I not hid.
I said, I will confess my transgressions unto the LORD;
and thou forgavest the iniquity of my sin. Selah.*
Psalms 32:5

There was once a man in the country of Syria who was the captain over all the armies of the country, but he had leprosy. His wife's little servant girl told him that the prophet in Israel (Elisha) could heal him of his leprosy, so Naaman took some gifts for the prophet and went to Israel to meet him. God miraculously healed Naaman, but the prophet Elisha refused to receive his gifts. But after Naaman started home, Elisha's servant, Gehazi, followed Naaman and made up a story to get Naaman to give him some of the gifts. Gehazi said that two young men had come to visit the prophet, and they needed some money and clothes for them. Naaman gave him what he asked for, and Gehazi went and hid the items in his house. When he got back to Elisha, God had already told Elisha what Gehazi had done. When Elisha questioned Gehazi, he lied to him. For lying, God punished Gehazi by letting him get sick with the leprosy that Naaman had been healed from.[76]

Have you sometimes made wrong choices, and then lied about them when you got caught? It is better to confess your wrongs to God and let Him forgive you because you cannot hide anything from Him.

Prayer: *Lord Jesus, the story about Gehazi is very frightening to me. Help me to always be honest about the wrong choices I make and ask you to forgive me. Teach me to choose right over wrong. Amen.*

Day #89 Don't Pray Fake Prayers

For the eyes of the Lord are over the righteous, and his ears are open unto their prayers: but the face of the Lord is against them that do evil.
1 Peter 3:12

---

[76] 2 Kings 5.

David ran from King Saul for over a year, and his prayers were desperate cries for God to protect him from death. God heard David's prayers, and in time, he became the second king over Israel. Saul on the other hand, prayed only when he got caught doing something wrong. He wasn't really sorry. He just wanted people to think he was doing the right thing. God doesn't listen to those kind of prayers, and in time, Saul died in battle, and his family lost the throne of Israel.

Prayer: *Lord Jesus, I want my heart to be right with you so you will listen to my prayers. Don't let me pray fake prayers like King Saul. Amen.*

Day #90   God Answers Earnest Prayer

Confess your faults one to another, and pray one for another, that ye may be healed. The effectual fervent prayer of a righteous man availeth much.
James 5:16

One of Israel's kings was named Ahab. He was very evil, and God decided to stop sending rain on Israel. The prophet Elijah found Ahab and told him it would not rain again until Elijah said so. Then Elijah went into hiding for three and a half years. When the time was up, he challenged the false prophets of Baal to a contest on top of Mt. Carmel. His prayer caused God to send fire from heaven to burn up the sacrifice on the altar. Then Elijah went off by himself and prayed earnestly until God sent rain upon Israel.[77] When you really have a need, God responds to earnest, fervent prayer.

Prayer: *Lord Jesus, let my prayers be fervent and sincere so that you will hear them and send the answers in Jesus' name. Amen.*

---

[77] 1 Kings 17-18. James 5:17-18.

Week 18 Review

Complete the crossword below

Across
4. Give us this day our daily ____.
7. Our Father, which art in ____.
8. ____ us from evil.
9. ____ us our debts, as we forgive our debtors.
12. Lead us not into ____.
14. Elijah's prayer brought ____ from heaven.

Down
1. Pray for others to be ____.
2. Thine is the kingdom and the ____ and the glory.
3. Gehazi ____ to Elisha and got punished.
5. Make your prayer requests with ____.
6. Thy ____ come. Thy will be done.
10. ____ your transgressions to the Lord.
11. Hallowed be thy ____.
13. God's ____ are open to the prayers of the righteous.

Memory Verse: Philippians 4:6 (Day #87)

Also memorize: The Lord's Prayer – Matthew 6:9-13 (Day #86)

Week 19

I Love My Church

Day #91   God Gives Pastors

And I will give you pastors according to mine heart,
which shall feed you with knowledge and understanding.
Jeremiah 3:15

The Old Testament prophet, Jeremiah wrote on several occasions that the pastors of Israel had forsaken God and had taught the Israelites to follow false gods. God was very angry with the pastors, but He promised Israel that He would give them new pastors. These pastors would love God and teach the Truth from God's Word to the people so they would understand exactly what they were supposed to do.

God wants you to have a pastor in your life, so you will also understand what you are supposed to do. He should be your very best friend because he will teach you how to get to Heaven.[78]

Prayer: *Lord Jesus, I pray that my pastor will always study your Word and teach me only true things from it so I will know how to live my life to please you. Amen.*

Day #92   Pray For Your Pastor

Obey them that have the rule over you, and submit yourselves: for they watch for
your souls, as they that must give account, that they may do it with joy, and not
with grief: for that is unprofitable for you. Pray for us: for we trust we have
a good conscience, in all things willing to live honestly.
Hebrews 13:17-18

God has put your pastor in charge of your soul. When he prays for all the people in his Church, he talks to God about you. Paul said to obey your pastor so that when he talks to God about you, he will be able to give God a good report for you. Because your pastor has so many people to pray for, you need to pray for him to be strong in teaching the Truth of God's Word and for God to protect him from anything that would influence him away from Truth like the pastors in Israel during Jeremiah's life.

---

[78] Ephesians 4:11-15.

Prayer: *Lord Jesus, thank you for a pastor who loves me and prays for me. Help him to stay strong in the Truth and be fearless in telling me what is right and wrong. Amen.*

Day #93   Attend Church Faithfully

Not forsaking the assembling of ourselves together, as the manner of some is; but exhorting one another: and so much the more, as ye see the day approaching.
Hebrews 10:25

Attending Church and Church activities should be the most important items in your weekly schedule. Paul said some people don't view Church attendance as very important. Don't be one of those people. The closer you get to the coming of the Lord, the more important it is to attend Church every time a service is scheduled. You need preaching, worship with your Church family and fellowship with those who believe like you do.

Prayer: *Lord Jesus, I'm thankful for my Church family. Help me to be faithful in attendance every week. Amen.*

Day #94   It's Church Time!

I was glad when they said unto me, Let us go into the house of the LORD.
Psalms 122:1

Do you wake up on Sunday mornings and say, "Yippee! It's Church day. I can't wait to get there!"? David said he was glad when someone told him it was time to go to the house of the Lord. Jesus is waiting for you to arrive so you can give Him praise, and you can hear His Word taught. The next time Church day rolls around, get excited about going to meet with Jesus and your Church family!

Prayer: *Lord Jesus, every day is a new day that you have given me to rejoice and be glad, but especially on Church days, I am happy I get to go to your house to praise you and learn more from your Word. Thank you for Church! Amen.*

Day #95   Sing To The Lord

Praise ye the LORD. I will praise the LORD with my whole heart,
in the assembly of the upright, and in the congregation.
Psalms 111:1

The praise and worship part of Church is your time to shine. More than sixty times the book of Psalms tells you to clap your hands and sing to the Lord. It is time to get excited about singing and praising Jesus with your whole heart. God loves to hear your praise to Him when you go to church.[79]

Prayer: *Lord Jesus, I love music about you, and I love to sing songs to you. Thank you for the gift of music in the Church. Amen.*

---

[79] Here are a few scriptures for more study about singing to the Lord: Psalms 7:17; 9:2; 13:6; 33:3; 47:1; 71:23; 81:1; 95:1; 98:4.

Week 19 Review

Fill in the blanks in the sentences below with the following words. (Hint: Not all words will be used.) behavior – church - clap - excited - gods – hands - house - Isaiah - Jeremiah - knowledge - leaders - listen - near - obey - pastors – praise – pray – preaches – report – shake – sing - Truth - understanding.

_____ wrote that Israel's pastors had taught Israel to follow false _____ . God sent _____ to Israel to feed them with _____ and _____. You should _____ your pastor because he has to give a _____ to God for your _____. Also _____ for him so he will always teach the _____. Try to attend _____ every time there is a service. Get _____ when it is time to go to God's _____. When you get to Church, _____ your _____ and _____ to the Lord. God comes _____ when His people _____ Him. Then _____ attentively when your pastor _____ God's Word.

Memory Verse: <u>Psalms 122:1</u> (Day #94)

Also memorize: <u>Psalms 100:1-5</u> - *Make a joyful noise unto the LORD, all ye lands.* ² *Serve the LORD with gladness: come before his presence with singing.* ³ *Know ye that the LORD he is God: it is he that hath made us, and not we ourselves; we are his people, and the sheep of his pasture.* ⁴ *Enter into his gates with thanksgiving, and into his courts with praise: be thankful unto him, and bless his name.* ⁵ *For the LORD is good; his mercy is everlasting; and his truth endureth to all generations.*

Week 20

Wise Words From The Apostle Paul

Paul instructing Timothy

Day #96   Respect Adults

Rebuke not an elder, but intreat him as a father; and the younger men as brethren; The elder women as mothers; the younger as sisters, with all purity. Honour widows that are widows indeed.
1 Timothy 5:1-3

Have you ever heard someone *smart off* to an adult, or have you done it yourself? Paul told Timothy that being disrespectful to an adult is wrong. Even if the adult is saying or doing something wrong, it is not the place of younger people to try to correct their elders. Elders, especially ministers,[80] should be treated with honor and respect. Widows also deserve to be honored and given a helping hand whenever you can do something nice for them. They often get lonely and need someone to help them do things around their home. As for people your own age, treat other boys and girls like you would want someone else to treat your brother or sister. You may argue with your siblings, but you get all protective if someone else mistreats them. Remember that, before you *smart off* to other boys and girls your age. Protect their feelings.

Prayer: *Lord Jesus, these instructions are pretty strong for someone who likes to speak up and prove they are right and others are wrong. Help me to listen to others' opinions and be polite and respectful when voicing my own opinions. And help me to especially notice widows or others who may be lonely, so I can offer to do something nice for them without being paid. Amen.*

Day #97   Avoid Arguments

But foolish and unlearned questions avoid, knowing that they do gender strifes. And the servant of the Lord must not strive; but be gentle unto all men, apt to teach, patient. In meekness instructing those that oppose themselves; if God peradventure will give them repentance to the acknowledging of the truth;
2 Timothy 2:23-25

Some people like to start arguments by saying things that hurt your feelings or make you mad. When the Apostle Paul wrote this letter to

---

[80] 1 Timothy 5:17.

young Timothy, he told him to stay away from people who enjoyed starting arguments or stirring up trouble. It is better to walk away or gently respond to them rather than getting caught up in the fuss and saying or doing something you will regret later. Besides, Paul said your gentle words may cause them to recognize their wrong and apologize for what they have done.

Prayer: *Lord Jesus, forgive me when I get caught up in heated arguments, and give me the strength I need to walk away from a fuss without saying a word or say only gentle words to the person. Amen.*

Day #98 Be Strong in Your Faith

Thou therefore, my son, be strong in the grace that is in Christ Jesus. And the things that thou hast heard of me among many witnesses, the same commit thou to faithful men, who shall be able to teach others also.
2 Timothy 2:1-2[81]

Little boys and girls often say they want to be strong like daddy or someone else they admire. Often they want you to see the strong muscles on their arm. Have you ever heard an adult say, "Just eat your Wheaties or your Cheerios and you will have strong muscles"? Of course, it takes more than just eating right to become strong. Exercise plays an important part in having a strong body that is able to walk, run, and jump without breaking a bone. But it is even more important to have a strong faith in the Lord so you can give answers for what you believe to anyone who challenges your faith.

How do you get strong in the faith? That strength comes from spending time in prayer and reading your Bible. It is not enough to just read it; you must think about it and study it until you have much of it memorized. Going to Church and listening to the preaching and teaching of pastors and Sunday School teachers will also strengthen your faith. Paul said to be strong and pass on the teachings that you have learned to others so they too can become strong in their faith.

---

[81] 1 Timothy 4:13-16; 2 Timothy 1:13-14.

Prayer: *Lord Jesus, why is it so easy to spend lots of time playing video games or watching a movie, but I fall asleep if I try to pray or read the Bible more than a few minutes? Help me to fall in love with your Word and find enjoyment in studying it and talking to you in prayer so I can share my faith with others who don't know you like I do. Amen.*

Day #99   Treasure Truth

> *O Timothy, keep that which is committed to thy trust, avoiding profane and vain babblings, and oppositions of science falsely so called: Which some professing have erred concerning the faith.*
> 1 Timothy 6:20-21

Young Timothy's dad was not a believer,[82] so Paul adopted Timothy as his son in the Gospel and taught him many things about living the Christian life. Timothy eventually became a preacher of the Gospel. Paul warned him to guard the teachings that had been given to him and to avoid godless people who would try to turn him away from his faith with their *so-called* knowledge.

People whose lives are not based on Bible teachings will lead you away from God. Don't listen to them. Guard the teachings of the Bible and even be willing to fight for the Truth,[83] for these truths are treasures that will lead you to Heaven.

Prayer: *Lord Jesus, I am thankful for my Bible. The words on its pages teach me how to please you. Help me to study it more so I can grow in my faith, and help me to boldly share my faith with others who do not know you. Amen.*

---

[82] Acts 16:1.
[83] 1 Timothy 1:18-19; 6:12-14; 2 Timothy 2:3-4.

Day #100   Finish the Race

*But continue thou in the things which thou hast learned
and hast been assured of, knowing of whom thou hast learned them;
And that from a child thou hast known the holy scriptures, which are
able to make thee wise unto salvation through faith which is in Christ Jesus.*
2 Timothy 3:14-15

Have you ever run in a race at school or with a group of friends? There are always more people who start the race than there are those who finish the race. Why doesn't everyone finish? Maybe they get tired and need a rest, or they get thirsty and stop to get a drink. Perhaps they trip and fall and have to leave the race. There are many reasons why some who start do not finish. Paul was very aware of this problem when he encouraged Timothy on two occasions[84] to continue believing and living the teachings of the Holy Scriptures that had been given to him from the time he was a small child. Knowledge of the scriptures helps you understand everything you need to do to be saved and live the Christian life that pleases Jesus.

Prayer: *Lord Jesus, this Christian race is one race that I intend to run all the way to the end. Help me to stay strong in my faith so I can finish well. Amen.*

---

[84] 1 Timothy 4:16.

Week 20 Review

Match the definitions on the left to the words on the right.

1. Treat them with honor and respect   ___ childhood

2. Treat elder women like a ____.   ___ faith

3. Give these ladies a helping hand.   ___ truth

4. Walk away from this.   ___ ministers

5. Bible reading and prayer builds strong ____.   ___ repent

6. Paul's son in the Gospel.   ___ widows

7. Bible truths will lead to ____.   ___ babblings

8. Timothy learned scriptures from ____.   ___ argument

9. This makes you wise unto salvation.   ___ Timothy

10. Avoid this.   ___ mothers

11. Be willing to fight for this.   ___ heaven

12. Gently teach others so they will ____.   ___ scriptures

Memory Verse: 2 Timothy 3:14-15 (Day #100)

Also memorize: Psalms 100:1-5 - Continue working on this Psalm.

> When you have learned all of Psalms 100, you have earned another day to celebrate hiding God's Word in your heart.

Week 21

The Joy Of Giving

Give Thanks

Day #101 Give Thanks

*Praise ye the LORD. O give thanks unto the LORD; for he is good:
for his mercy endureth for ever.*
Psalms 106:1

Do you feel disappointed if you do something nice for someone, and they don't even say thank you? Children with good manners learn to say "please" when they ask for something, and "thank you" any time someone gives them something. In the same way, God is looking for people who will give Him praise and thanks for the things He does for them every day.[85] He gives you life, a place to sleep, food to eat, and clothes to wear. If you made a list of things that God does for you every day, it would be very, very long. Start a new habit of giving praise and thanks to God every day, throughout the day. God will love it, and developing an attitude of gratitude will make you feel better.

Prayer: *Lord Jesus, you do so many wonderful things for me every day. I want to say thank you today for family and friends, the gift of music and singing, and my treasured Bible. Amen.*

Day #102 Give Money

*Honour the LORD with thy substance, and with the firstfruits
of all thine increase: So shall thy barns be filled with plenty,
and thy presses shall burst out with new wine.*
Proverbs 3:9-10

God doesn't need your money because He owns everything. Instead, He asks you to develop the habit of unselfishly giving money to support the Church and help those who are in need. He promises a blessing to those who give a tithe (ten percent) of all their income.[86] If you get $1 for taking out the trash, then $.10 goes to God. When my children were young, they took their tithes out of their allowance as soon as we gave it to them, and they kept it in a tithes jar in their bedroom. When they had collected several dollars, they would bring it to church in an envelope and put it in

---

[85] Additional scriptures for giving thanks and praise: Psalms 18:49; 30:4; 35:18; 57:7; 92:1; 108:1; 1 Thessalonians 5:18.
[86] Malachi 3:8-11.

the offering. If you will learn to give generously to God and others, God will see to it that others give to you in your time of need.[87]

Prayer: *Lord Jesus, I need to work on this area of giving. When I work hard to earn money, I usually have something in mind that I want to buy with it. Teach me to give first to your cause, and save some for others before I spend it all on myself. Amen.*

Day #103   Give Time

But a certain Samaritan, as he journeyed, came where he was: and when he saw him, he had compassion on him, And went to him, and bound up his wounds, pouring in oil and wine, and set him on his own beast, and brought him to an inn, and took care of him.
Luke 10:33-34

Jesus told a story one day about a man who was traveling alone, and some thieves who were hiding beside the road jumped out and beat him. They stole everything he had, then left him almost dead along the roadside. Several religious leaders passed by and saw the man, but didn't want to get involved. Finally, a Samaritan who was a stranger, passed by and had compassion for the injured man. He stopped, cleaned his wounds, and put bandages on them. Then he helped the man get on his horse, brought him to an inn and took care of him. When he had to leave the man, he gave money to the innkeeper to care for the man until he got well. Jesus praised the stranger for his kind deed to a man he didn't even know.[88]

Think of ways you could give time to someone. You could offer to read to a younger sibling or play a game with them. Maybe you could offer to help your neighbor in his yard or sweep the leaves off the driveway without pay. Try to think of some way to give time to someone who needs help.

Prayer: *Lord Jesus, I enjoy spending my free time doing what I want to do, but I know you are pleased when I do something helpful for someone else. Help me to pay attention to needs around me and volunteer to be a good helper. Amen.*

---

[87] Luke 6:38.
[88] To read the whole story of the Good Samaritan see: Luke 10:25-37.

Day #104   Give Knowledge

Give instruction to a wise man, and he will be yet wiser:
teach a just man, and he will increase in learning.
Proverbs 9:9

How many times have you seen someone struggling to do something that you know how to do well, but you didn't offer to help them? Perhaps a younger child was trying to tie his shoes, but he kept getting the laces tangled up. When we give of our knowledge to someone else, Solomon said that person will increase in their learning. When you teach someone how to do something, then you feel good for being a helper, and they feel happy that they don't have to ask for help anymore. Think about the things you know how to do well and try to find someone to share your knowledge with today.

Prayer: *Lord Jesus, lead me to someone today who could benefit from knowledge that I could share with them. Amen.*

Day #105   Give Ear to God

He that hath an ear, let him hear what the Spirit saith unto the churches.
Revelation 2:29

There are many voices that speak to you every day. They may speak through music or through an electronic game you are playing. Perhaps the voice is the cry of a hungry baby or the laughing voices of children at play. Sometimes you may put on headphones to tune out the voices you don't want to hear. God speaks every day also, but we have to listen for His voice. Sometimes He speaks through His Word, and sometimes He speaks through your pastor or another minister. At other times He may speak through worship music, or He may just speak a thought into your mind. However God chooses to speak to you, just give ear to what He has to say and then obey everything He tells you to do.

Prayer: *Lord Jesus, help me to tune out the many voices from everyday life and listen closely to hear whatever you have to say to me today. Amen.*

Week 21 Review

Find the following words in the grid below.

Attitude – Clothes - Compassion – Ear - God - Gratitude – Hear - Helper - Income – Innkeeper – Instruction - Knowledge – Learning - Mercy – Obey – Plenty – Samaritan - Spirit - Thanks – Thought – Tithes

H	N	J	Z	K	N	O	W	L	E	D	G	E	N	B	Y
L	D	P	L	H	O	O	W	K	U	Q	K	G	A	A	S
H	O	M	G	R	F	P	I	Y	B	U	A	S	T	A	K
O	Z	V	A	R	E	D	U	T	I	T	T	A	I	H	N
Q	J	E	X	N	A	Y	B	X	C	P	L	X	R	Y	A
U	H	N	C	R	S	T	H	V	D	U	H	A	A	E	H
A	B	O	Y	P	E	X	I	E	Q	V	R	R	M	B	T
S	T	I	T	H	E	S	A	T	L	E	E	T	A	O	R
P	L	S	T	V	J	R	L	F	U	P	B	Y	S	I	G
I	E	S	E	H	T	O	L	C	E	D	E	C	Q	N	R
R	A	A	M	R	O	A	Q	E	Z	X	E	R	N	C	I
I	R	P	I	B	V	U	K	Y	E	P	V	E	G	O	D
T	N	M	N	O	E	N	G	A	J	E	U	M	K	M	M
U	I	O	Y	H	N	H	B	H	D	V	S	L	J	E	M
T	N	C	S	I	T	Z	D	L	T	G	S	B	J	H	F
R	G	B	X	Y	T	N	E	L	P	L	R	Z	Q	B	B

Memory Verse: Proverbs 3:9-10 (Day #102)

Also memorize: Luke 6:38 - *Give, and it shall be given unto you; good measure, pressed down, and shaken together, and running over, shall men give into your bosom. For with the same measure that ye mete withal it shall be measured to you again.*

Week 22

Fruit Of The Spirit (Part 1)

Bethany

Day #106 — Fruit of the Spirit

*But the **fruit of the Spirit** is love, joy, peace, longsuffering, gentleness, goodness, faith, Meekness, temperance: against such there is no law.*
Galatians 5:22-23

The first proof that a person has been filled with the Spirit is the sign of speaking in tongues. The way a person changes and acts after being filled with the Spirit are continued proofs that the Spirit is living inside. As the Fruit of the Spirit grows in your life, it becomes easier for you to do the right thing. There is no law that can rule against the Fruit of the Spirit working in your life.

Prayer: *Lord Jesus, let my life become a fruitful tree that produces the Fruit of your Spirit so that others can see that you are living in me. Amen.*

Day #107 — Fruit of Love

*Let **love** be without dissimulation. Abhor that which is evil; cleave to that which is good. Be kindly affectioned one to another with brotherly love; in honour preferring one another;*
Romans 12:9-10

The words "dissimulation" and "abhor" may be unfamiliar to you. To help you understand better, the scripture means, don't pretend to *love* someone if you can't stand them. Hate everything that is evil, but hold on tightly to everything that is good. *Love* everyone like you do your own family or best friend, and show honor by giving them the best treatment. For example, you could tell someone else to take your seat while you stand, or you could offer to do something nice for someone without getting paid to do it. Jesus said that people in the world would recognize that you are His disciple by the *love* that you show toward others. Practice making the fruit of *love* a part of your everyday activity.

Prayer: *Lord Jesus, let my love for others be honest and sincere. Help me to think of others' needs before my own and be helpful to others in any way I can so that others can see your **love** at work in my life. Amen.*

Day #108   Fruit of Joy

*Thou wilt shew me the path of life: in thy presence is fulness of **joy**;*
at thy right hand there are pleasures for evermore.
Psalms 16:11

Joy is a deep feeling of calm delight in your God. The way to grow the fruit of ***joy*** in your life is to spend time in God's presence through prayer and study of His Word. Schedule those times of refreshing every day.

Prayer: *Lord Jesus, sometimes it seems like reading the Bible is not as interesting as reading other books, and it is sometimes hard to talk to someone I can't see. As I obey your instructions to pray and study Your Word, give me a big hug and let the **joy** of the Lord fill my heart. Amen.*

Day #109   Fruit of Peace

***Peace** I leave with you, my **peace** I give unto you:*
not as the world giveth, give I unto you.
Let not your heart be troubled, neither let it be afraid.
John 14:27

One day Jesus and His disciples got in a boat to travel to a different place. Jesus was tired and immediately fell asleep. A storm suddenly arose on the sea, and the disciples became very frightened because the wind was blowing the waves so high that water began filling the boat. The disciples woke Jesus and told Him they were going to die in the storm, but Jesus was not afraid. He calmly commanded the wind to stop blowing and told the sea, "***Peace**, be still.*" The wind and the sea instantly obeyed His voice, and the storm was over.[89] Remember this story the next time you are afraid. Just cry out to Jesus, and He will bring the fruit of ***peace*** and calm back into your heart.

Prayer: *Lord Jesus, it is a comfort to know that you are the peace-giver. When I am afraid, I will trust you to calm my fears and speak **peace** to my heart. Amen.*

---

[89] Mark 4:35-41

Day #110   Fruit of Longsuffering

I ...beseech you that ye walk worthy of the vocation
wherewith ye are called, With all lowliness and meekness,
*with **longsuffering**, forbearing one another in love;*
Endeavouring to keep the unity of the Spirit in the bond of peace.
Ephesians 4:1-3

Paul taught the Church at Ephesus that they needed to live their lives in such a way that others would recognize that they were a Christian. Some of those traits were humility and gentleness. He further instructed them to patiently put up with others even when they irritated them. If the fruit of **longsuffering** (which is another word for patience) can grow in your life, it will help you to live in harmony and peace with others in the Church.

Prayer: *Lord Jesus, sometimes I get impatient with others who annoy me or say something hurtful to someone else. In those times of annoyance, let me remember to think before I speak, and when I speak, let my words be spoken in gentleness and love. Amen.*

Week 22 Review

Unscramble the 9 Fruit of the Spirit.

1. ogsnoeds   _____

2. capee   _____

3. nesmekse   _____

4. gestleenns   _____

5. evol   _____

6. eetmanerpc   _____

7. yoj   _____

8. iftha   _____

9. fnlgugosfnrie   _____

Memory Verse: Galatians 5:22-23 (Day #106)

Also memorize: Philippians 4:7 - *And the peace of God, which passeth all understanding, shall keep your hearts and minds through Christ Jesus.*

Week 23

Fruit Of The Spirit (Part 2)

Day #111   Fruit of Gentleness

To speak evil of no man, to be no brawlers,
*but **gentle**, shewing all meekness unto all men.*
Titus 3:2

Aaron was the new boy in school. He was always dressed neatly, but his clothes were not expensive or even the most current styles. The boys in his class laughed at his odd clothes and would not invite him to join them at lunch or at recess. Aaron would go home and cry each day. One day Brad told his mother about the new boy who looked odd and didn't fit in with his friends. His mother suggested that Brad do something nice for Aaron the next day and try to get to know him. So, Brad brought extra snacks in his lunch the next day. He asked Aaron to sit by him at lunch, and they began talking about things that interested them. Soon Brad brought out the extra snack and gave it to Aaron. After several days of eating lunch with Aaron, Brad realized that Aaron was a very nice boy, and he was sorry that he had joined the other boys in their class by teasing Aaron and making fun of his clothes. Because of Brad's **gentleness**, he and Aaron soon became best friends.

Titus taught that we should not say cruel things to others or get into arguments with them. Everyone deserves to be shown **gentleness** and kindness.

Prayer: *Lord Jesus, when others dress oddly or talk funny, let the fruit of **gentleness** cause me to be kind and **gentle** with them until I get to know them better. Amen.*

Day #112   Fruit of Goodness

And I myself also am persuaded of you, my brethren,
*that ye also are full of **goodness**, filled with all knowledge,*
able also to admonish one another.
Romans 15:14

How do you feel when you bring home your report card, and you have earned an "A" in every one of your classes? Do you feel glad that you studied and worked hard to learn the information so you could do well on your tests? When your parents praise you for doing a *good* job, does that make you want to work hard the next quarter so they will praise you again?

Paul complimented the people in the Church at Rome and told them they were full of **goodness** and knowledge and knew how to gently caution others to do well. The fruit of **goodness** will help you to get along with others and to do well in your studies.

Prayer: *Lord Jesus, it makes me feel* **good** *when others praise me for the* **good** *things I do. Help the fruit of* **goodness** *to continue growing in my heart so that others can see that I belong to you. Amen.*

Day #113 Fruit of Faith

> *So then* **faith** *cometh by hearing,*
> *and hearing by the word of God.*
> Romans 10:17

One day Jesus was teaching His disciples about trusting in Him to take care of their needs of food, clothing, and a place to sleep. He scolded them for worrying about these matters and told them they only had a little bit of **faith**.[90] How does a person get more **faith** to believe Jesus will take care of them? Jesus told the disciples to seek the Kingdom of God first and His righteousness, and all the other things they needed would be given to them. Paul taught the Church at Rome that **faith** came by hearing the Word of God. So, the more you hear and obey the Word, the more the fruit of **faith** grows in your heart.

Prayer: *Lord Jesus, I don't want to be scolded for having little* **faith**. *I want to pay attention to my pastor when he preaches and to my Sunday School teachers when they teach, and I especially want to pay attention to my daily devotions at home with my parents so that the fruit of* **faith** *will grow in my heart. Amen.*

---

[90] Matthew 6:25-34

Day #114   Fruit of Meekness

> *...follow after righteousness, godliness, faith, love, patience, **meekness**.*
> 1 Timothy 6:11

Have you ever played "Follow the Leader"? Everyone who follows the leader has to do exactly what the leader does or tells them to do, and they have to go where the leader goes, or tells them to go. As a Christian, you must be careful who you follow. Paul said to follow him as he followed Christ.[91] It is important to follow a Godly role model who can lead you to do right, live Godly, and grow in faith, love, patience, and ***meekness***.

Prayer: *Lord Jesus, I want the **Fruit of the Spirit** to grow in my life. Help me to follow Godly men and women who will teach me your ways. Amen.*

Day #115   Fruit of Temperance

> *... add to your faith virtue; and to virtue knowledge; And to knowledge **temperance**; and to temperance patience; and to patience godliness; And to godliness brotherly kindness; and to brotherly kindness charity.*
> 2 Peter 1:5-7

In Peter's letter to the Church, he described some building blocks to help you grow in your Christian faith. He said to start with the block of faith, then place a block of goodness on top of it. Next, he added a block of learning new things. Then he added the block of temperance (or self-control). On top of that block came the block of patience, then the block of kindness, and finally, the top block of the building was love. Peter went on to say that if you had all of these building blocks in your life, you would produce *fruit* that would let other people know that you are a Christian.

Prayer: *Lord Jesus, thank you for your Word that guides me in building my life on the proper foundation of faith and Godly values. Every day I am learning more about you and trying to become more like you. Help me to have self-control and instead of demanding things be done my way to get what I want. Thank you for all the Godly people who are helping me on this journey. Amen.*

---

[91] 1 Corinthians 11:1

Week 23 Review

Answer True or False for each statement below.

_____ 1. You should speak evil about others.

_____ 2. Show meekness to all men.

_____ 3. Paul praised the people in Ephesus for their goodness.

_____ 4. People of Rome were filled with all knowledge.

_____ 5. Faith comes by hearing praise singing.

_____ 6. Jesus said to seek the Kingdom of God first.

_____ 7. The fruit of faith grows when you obey the Word.

_____ 8. Paul said to follow him as he followed other leaders.

_____ 9. Peter said to add virtue and knowledge to your faith.

_____ 10. The final fruit that should be added to faith is charity.

Memory Verse: Romans 10:17 (Day #113)

Also memorize: Hebrews 11:6 - *But without faith it is impossible to please him: for he that cometh to God must believe that he is, and that he is a rewarder of them that diligently seek him.*

Week 24

Growing Fruits Of Righteousness (Part 1)

Day #116   Be Considerate

Let no man seek his own, but every man another's wealth.
1 Corinthians 10:24

What does it mean to seek wealth or well-being for someone else before you seek it for yourself? Let me illustrate with a story.

Joey and Johnny had been best friends from the day they both entered kindergarten together. They were in the same classes and spent a lot of time in each other's homes. When they were in sixth grade, a writing contest was announced. The winner of the contest would represent the school in the state writing tournament. Both boys entered the contest and wrote excellent stories. Each one was certain that his story would be chosen to represent their school. Johnny had never traveled much, so this was an opportunity for him to experience something new and exciting. Joey, on the other hand, had visited many other cities with his parents, so a trip to the state competition wasn't a totally new adventure for him. On the day that the winners were announced, there was a tie between Joey and Johnny. Another set of judges would have to review their stories to break the tie, but before new judges could be appointed, Joey stepped up and asked that the honor be given to his friend Johnny. Yes, Joey wanted to win the contest as much as Johnny did, but he unselfishly stepped down so that his friend could experience the fun of representing their school. Joey's teachers and parents were proud of his decision to let Johnny win the contest, but God was more pleased because Joey demonstrated the Bible teaching of being unselfish and helping someone else receive a blessing.

Prayer: *Lord Jesus, the world teaches us to be competitive and do whatever it takes to win, but help me to remember that you are pleased when I decide to willingly step aside from receiving something I really want so that someone else can receive it instead.*

Day #117   Be Merciful

Blessed are the merciful: for they shall obtain mercy.
Matthew 5:7

Jesus told a story about a man who owed the king $60,000. The king brought the man in and demanded that he pay all of his debt right then. The man begged for mercy because he didn't have the money, so the king felt sorry for him and forgave the whole debt. The man immediately went out and found one of his friends who only owed him one dime. He grabbed the man by the throat and demanded that he pay him right then. The second man begged for forgiveness, but the evil man who had just been forgiven a much larger debt, refused to show mercy. He had his friend put into jail. When the king heard what the first man had done, he was very angry and asked him why he couldn't forgive the small amount his friend owed him after the king had forgiven him such a huge amount. The king then threw the first man into prison.[92] Jesus said if we will have mercy on other people, He will have mercy on us.

Prayer: *Lord Jesus, help me to be merciful to others who have wronged me so that I can receive mercy from you when I make wrong choices. Amen*

Day #118   Be Unselfish

Look not every man on his own things,
but every man also on the things of others.
Philippians 2:4

Selfishness is part of human nature. You want to take care of yourself before you take care of others. Little children have to be taught to share their toys with others. God's Word teaches you to be concerned not only about our own possessions or needs, but also to notice if others are in need, and if they are, you are to share with them.

Prayer: *Lord Jesus, sometimes I want more stuff when I already have enough games, toys, food, clothes, and a nice place to live. Help me to be more aware of*

---

[92] Matthew 19:23-35

others' needs and be willing to give to them, even if it means I can't always get what I want. Amen.

Day #119 — Do Good Works

> *But to do good and to communicate forget not: for with such sacrifices God is well pleased.*
> Hebrews 13:16[93]

Many American children have more toys and electronic gadgets than they can play with. They often get bored with their playthings when the newness wears off. How many toys, games, and gadgets do you own that you no longer enjoy playing with? Doing good things for others and sharing is an important Bible teaching. Find someone who doesn't have as much and share some of your abundance with them. Or better yet, select one of your toys that you really like and give it to someone who doesn't have one. That kind of sacrifice is very pleasing to God.

Prayer: *Lord Jesus, I have been given so much, and sometimes I am ungrateful for what I have because of my desire to get something new. Help me to be thankful for what I have and be willing to share of my abundance with others who don't have as much.*

Day #120 — Forgive

> *Take heed to yourselves: If thy brother trespass against thee, rebuke him; and if he repent, forgive him.*
> Luke 17:3[94]

If someone hurts your feelings or harms you in any way, tell them what they did wrong, and if they tell you they are sorry, accept their apology and forgive them. Forgiveness means that you don't keep reminding them or telling others what they did against you. When you forgive as God does, He casts your sins into the depths of the sea[95] so they can't be used against

---

[93] See also: Galatians 6:9.
[94] See also: Ephesians 4:31-32; Colossians 3:12-14.
[95] Micah 7:19.

you ever again. Sometimes it is hard to forget hurtful things that others do to you, but God will help you to learn to forgive the way He does.

Prayer: *Lord Jesus, teach me to let go of grudges and hard feelings against someone who has done me wrong and has asked for forgiveness. Let me learn to forgive others in the same way that you have forgiven me.*

Week 24 Review

Complete the crossword below

Across
3. Lots of money or possessions.
4. Generous and giving to others.
7. To sin against God.
8. A public officer who rules on court cases.
11. To pardon someone who mistreated you.
12. Showing kindness to someone.

Down
1. ___ your toys and games with others.
2. Say this before you eat your food.
5. To give up something that you really enjoy.
6. A written expression of sorrow for wrongdoing.
9. One who wins the prize.
10. Saying you are sorry.

Memory Verse: Matthew 5:7 (Day #117)

Also memorize: Galatians 6:9 - *And let us not be weary in well doing: for in due season we shall reap, if we faint not.*

Week 25

Growing Fruits Of Righteousness (Part 2)

Day #121   Love Others

If ye fulfil the royal law according to the scripture,
Thou shalt love thy neighbour as thyself, ye do well:
James 2:8

The Bible tells us that loving others as much as we love our self is a royal law. Do you know what a royal law is? It is a law that is made by someone who is a king or queen. Since they are the rulers over the people, they have the right to make the laws for people to obey. Did you know that God is the highest King over every other king or queen on earth, so His laws are stronger than the laws of earthly kings? God is very serious about loving other people as much as you love yourself, for His Word teaches about loving others dozens of times. If you can learn to love your bratty brother or sister as much as yourself, God will give you a "Well Done" report.

Prayer: *Lord Jesus, sometimes my brother, sister, or cousins irritate me to the point that I want to tell them off or hit them. Help me to love them like you love me, and give love instead of sharp words or actions. Amen.*

Day #122   Make Right Choices

Therefore to him that knoweth to do good, and doeth it not, to him it is sin.
James 4:17

What is the definition of sin? The dictionary says that sin is a willful act of disobedience against the laws of God. We may think of sin as something big like disobeying one of the Ten Commandments, but James tells us that if we know what we are supposed to do and don't do it, that is a sin. Let me give you some easy examples. Suppose your parents instruct you to take the trash out to the curb every Friday, but one Friday you decide to do other things first, and you willfully decided not to obey your parents instruction. You just sinned because you knew what you were to do, but didn't do it. Maybe it might be your job to clear the table and wipe it off after every meal, but one night you have a friend visiting you, and you get up from the table and go out to play without doing your job. So, your mom has to do it. You just sinned because you didn't do what you knew you were supposed to do. Be careful about neglecting to do the good things that are expected of you.

Prayer: *Lord Jesus, I want to be a good person, so help me to remember to do the things I know I am supposed to do, and when I forget or neglect to do them, help me to repent and do better next time.*

Day #123   Say Right Words

*Let the words of my mouth, and the meditation of my heart,
be acceptable in thy sight, O LORD, my strength, and my redeemer.*
Psalms 19:14

Jesus taught a lesson one day about the words people say. He said whatever you think about will eventually come out of your mouth. If you think mean and hateful thoughts, you will say mean and hateful words, but if you think kind and pleasant thoughts, you will say kind and pleasant words.[96] The writer of Psalms 19 prayed for his words and his thoughts to be acceptable to God. It is a good idea to pray this verse every morning when you wake up.

Prayer: *Lord Jesus, as I start this new day, let my thoughts and my words be pleasing to you. I want my words to honor you. Amen.*

Day #124   Serve Wholeheartedly

*And whatsoever ye do, do it heartily, as to the Lord, and not unto men;
Knowing that of the Lord ye shall receive the reward of the inheritance:
for ye serve the Lord Christ.*
Colossians 3:23-24

There was a little Jewish girl in the Bible who was captured in a war with the Syrians, and she became a servant for the wife of Naaman, who was the chief captain of Syria's armies. We don't even know the young girl's name, but apparently she accepted her situation and worked for Naaman's wife without complaining. Naaman was afflicted with the dreaded disease of leprosy, and the little servant girl witnessed to her captors about the healing power of Israel's God. She said if only Naaman could go to the prophet in Israel, he would be healed. Naaman did go, and he did receive

---

[96] Matthew 12:34-37.

his healing because of a little unnamed girl who did her job well in a strange country among idol-worshippers.[97]

Can you do your chores around the house without complaining? Sometimes your good deeds may not get noticed, but God is watching, and in time, He will reward all your efforts to do good during your lifetime.

Prayer: *Lord Jesus, forgive me when I complain about doing my chores, or sometimes I do them sloppily just to get them over with. Help me to try harder to do everything to the best of my ability because you are watching and keeping records of my activities and my attitude. Amen.*

Day #125   Think Right Thoughts

Finally, brethren, whatsoever things are true, whatsoever things are honest, whatsoever things are just, whatsoever things are pure, whatsoever things are lovely, whatsoever things are of good report; if there be any virtue, and if there be any praise, think on these things.
Philippians 4:8

What kind of things do you think about throughout the day? The wise King Solomon said we are what we think.[98] If you think about happy things, you will be happy, but if you think about things that anger you, you will act angry toward someone else.

Richard Wurmbrand was a preacher from Romania during World War 2. Russia took over his country after the War and arrested Rev. Wurmbrand for his Christian beliefs. He spent fourteen years in prison, and much of that time, the jailers beat and tortured him to try and make him give up his Christian faith. He never gave up what he believed.[99] How do you think he survived through fourteen years of mistreatment? He made up his mind to think about things that were true, honest, just, pure, lovely, of good report, virtuous, and praiseworthy. He could have hated his captors during all those years, but he chose to think on the goodness of God and recall promises from God's Word. The next time you are having a bad day, try to

---

[97] 2 Kings 5:1-15.
[98] Proverbs 23:7.
[99] Richard Wurmbrand. "Tortured For Christ," (Bartlesville, OK: Living Sacrifice Book Company, 1967).

change your thoughts and watch God change your attitude to one of gratitude for His love and goodness to you.

Prayer: *Lord Jesus, I have never been persecuted for being a Christian. After reading about what Rev. Wurmbrand went through, my problems seem small in comparison to his. Help me to guard my thoughts and practice thinking about things that will keep a praise on my lips for all the good things you do for me each day. Amen.*

Week 25 Review

Number from 1-15 the phrases from the five verses in this week's lessons. Number them in the same order that you studied them.

____If ye fulfil the royal law according to the scripture,

____Therefore to him that knoweth to do good,

____Let the words of my mouth, and the meditation of my heart,

____And whatsoever ye do, do it heartily, as to the Lord,

____Finally, brethren, whatsoever things are true,

____whatsoever things are of good report; if there be any virtue,

____and doeth it not, to him it is sin.

____be acceptable in thy sight, O LORD, my strength, and my redeemer.

____and if there be any praise, think on these things.

____and not unto men; Knowing that of the Lord

____whatsoever things are pure, whatsoever things are lovely,

____ye shall receive the reward of the inheritance:

____Thou shalt love thy neighbour as thyself, ye do well:

____whatsoever things are honest, whatsoever things are just,

____for ye serve the Lord Christ.

Memory Verse: All 5 verses for this week. James 2:8 (Day #121); James 4:17 (Day #122); Psalms 19:14 (Day #123); Colossians 3:23-24 (Day #124); Philippians 4:8 (Day #125).

Week 26

Be A Hard Worker

Day #126 Four Wise Creatures

There be four things which are little upon the earth, but they are exceeding wise: The ants are a people not strong, yet they prepare their meat in the summer; The conies are but a feeble folk, yet make they their houses in the rocks; The locusts have no king, yet go they forth all of them by bands; The spider taketh hold with her hands, and is in kings' palaces.
Proverbs 30:24-28

It is easy to make excuses for not being a hard worker. *Your foot hurts. You are not strong enough. It's not your turn to do it.* But Solomon gives us an example of four little creatures who accomplish big things in spite of many obstacles that try to block them. Although ants and locusts are small, they work together like a huge army to prepare food for the winter. Conies are little guinea pigs that have learned to hide in places that are not easily reached by their enemies. Spiders have determination to get wherever they want to go even when they are not wanted. So, what is your excuse? Teamwork and determination will get the job done.

Prayer: *Lord Jesus, forgive me for making excuses when I don't want to get my chores done. Help me to just make up my mind to do what I'm asked to do and ask for help if the job is too big for me to handle by myself. Amen.*

Day #127 Hard Workers Are Blessed

The soul of the sluggard desireth, and hath nothing: but the soul of the diligent shall be made fat.
Proverbs 13:4

There are two words in this verse that we need to define to help us understand what Solomon is teaching us. A *sluggard* is someone who is lazy, but someone who is *diligent* works hard and does their work well. From this verse we learn that lazy people want to have nice things, but because they are too lazy to work for them, they have nothing. On the other hand, God abundantly blesses those who work hard and do a good job. Do you want God's favor? Then be a hard worker.

Prayer: *Lord Jesus, help me to learn the value of hard work while I am young so that when I grow up, I will gladly work to earn money to pay for the things I need and want rather than expecting others to buy things for me. Amen.*

Day #128   Do Your Work Well

*Whatsoever thy hand findeth to do, do it with thy might;
for there is no work, nor device, nor knowledge, nor wisdom,
in the grave, whither thou goest.*
Ecclesiastes 9:10

This verse was one of my Sunday School memory verses when I was about eight or nine years old. My Sunday School teacher got us all excited about looking around our world and finding things to do without being asked. I remember going home, and for several days, I tried to notice things I could do to help my mother without her asking me. The Bible teaches us to do all our work to the very best of our ability because when our life is over, there won't be any more work for us to do. We will be remembered for the good things we did while we were alive.

Prayer: *Lord Jesus, when I get tired of doing chores day-in and day-out, help me to remember that you are pleased when I do my chores well without complaining.*

Day #129   Hard Work is God's Gift

*And also that every man should eat and drink,
and enjoy the good of all his labour, it is the gift of God.*
Ecclesiastes 3:13

Hard work is a gift from God? God knew from the beginning that our bodies needed to lift and tug and push in order to become strong. He told the very first man Adam, that he would have to make a living for his family by the sweat of his face.[100] If you want to be strong and healthy, you must move your body every day. Do whatever is necessary to get your school work and your chores done each day. When you grow up and get a job earning money, be the very best worker you can be. Then when you sit down to your table to eat food, you can be happy that you have worked

---

[100] Genesis 3:17-19.

hard and helped to buy the things that you need. The satisfaction you feel for a job well done is God's gift to you.

Prayer: *Lord Jesus, sometimes I am so tired that I don't want to do another chore. And sometimes I would rather play with my electronic games than do chores for mom. Help me to understand that hard work gives me the satisfaction of helping mom and others. Thank you for this gift. Amen.*

Day #130   No Stealing Allowed

Let him that stole steal no more: but rather let him labour,
working with his hands the thing which is good,
that he may have to give to him that needeth.
Ephesians 4:28

Apparently the Church at Ephesus had some members who were converted from their past life of stealing. They had to be taught that stealing was not the proper way to get money. Paul taught that everyone should work with their hands to earn money to pay for the necessary things they needed. Then rather than use extra money to buy more *stuff*, Paul taught that we should give our extra money to others who were in need. Don't spend all the money you earn for your own wants. It is better to save some to share with others who don't have as much.

Prayer: *Lord Jesus, it is easy to become selfish with the money that I work hard to earn. Help me to be content with using enough to take care of my needs and save a little extra to share with others too. Amen.*

Week 26 Review

Answer True or False for each statement below.

____ 1. Ants are strong and work hard in the winter time.

____ 2. Conies are weak and live among the rocks.

____ 3. Locusts are led by a king.

____ 4. Spiders use their feet to get inside palaces.

____ 5. Teamwork and determination helps get your work done.

____ 6. Lazy people get everything they want without working for it.

____ 7. God blesses those who are diligent in their work.

____ 8. Do all your work to the best of your ability.

____ 9. The satisfaction you feel when you work hard is God's gift to you.

____ 10. Stealing is a better way to make money than working for it.

____ 11. Paul taught people to share their extra things with others.

____ 12. If you work hard, you deserve to keep everything for yourself.

Memory Verse: Ephesians 4:28 (Day #130)

Additional Memory Verses: Romans 12:10-13:
[10] *Be kindly affected one to another with brotherly love; in honour preferring one another;*
[11] *Not slothful in business; fervent in spirit; serving the Lord;*
[12] *Rejoicing in hope; patient in tribulation; continuing instant in prayer;*
[13] *Distributing to the necessity of saints; given to hospitality.*

Week 27

Be A Godly Example

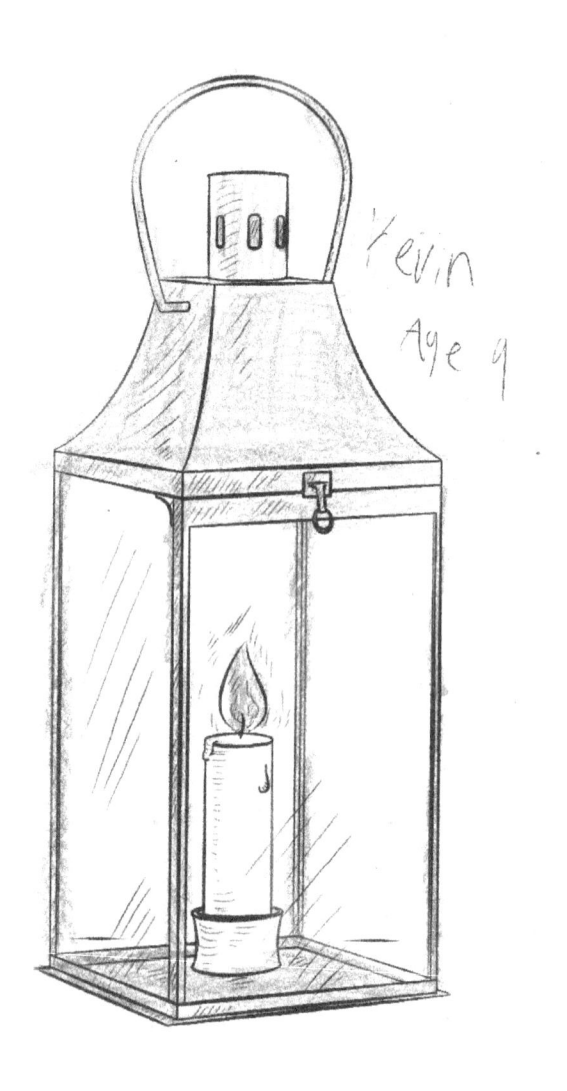

Let Your Light Shine For Jesus

160

Day #131 Enjoy Your Youth

Let no man despise thy youth; but be thou an example of the believers, in word, in conversation, in charity, in spirit, in faith, in purity.
1 Timothy 4:12

Have you ever said, "I wish I was twelve so I could join the youth group at Church," or "I wish I was sixteen so I could drive"? I too remember wanting to be sixteen so I could drive, and eighteen so I could be out of school. It is tempting to look ahead at others who are older and wish we could hurry and be that age so we could have more privileges. The Apostle Paul cautioned young Timothy against wishing away his youth so he could do things that grown-ups do. He said young people can be examples of a believer by the way they talk and love others. They can also be full of the Spirit of God, full of faith, and lead a pure life. Go ahead and show the world that you can be a Christian while you are young. Lead the way so others can follow your example.

Prayer: *Lord Jesus, help me to enjoy each day of my life as a child and a young adult. I want others to see that I am a true believer by the Godly way I live my life. Amen.*

Day #132 Let Your Light Shine

Let your light so shine before men, that they may see your good works, and glorify your Father which is in heaven.
Matthew 5:16

Jesus said He is the Light of the world, and those who follow Him will walk in His life-giving light.[101] But it gets better than that! When Jesus comes into your heart and fills you with the Holy Ghost, His light lives in you and shines out of you so that everyone can see that you are God's child. Then you can obey His teaching to be a light to the world so others can see your good works and give glory to God.[102] Be a bright light for Jesus in this dark world of sin.

---

[101] John 8:12.
[102] Matthew 5:14-16.

Prayer: *Lord Jesus, thank you for being light in my life. Help me to shine your light brightly for everyone to see you living in me.*

Day #133   Take Advice Cheerfully

The way of a fool is right in his own eyes:
but he that hearkeneth unto counsel is wise.
Proverbs 12:15

We often think we are old enough to make our own choices and don't need anyone to tell us what to do, but the Bible says people who think like that are fools. The dictionary uses the words *blockhead, ignoramus,* or *moron* to describe a fool. Nobody wants to be called those words. The wise and smart thing to do is to listen to advice from your parents and others who are older than you.

Prayer: *Lord Jesus, help me to remember that I don't know it all yet, so I need to listen to others who have lived longer than I have. Amen.*

Day #134   Enjoy Learning New Things

The fear of the LORD is the beginning of knowledge:
but fools despise wisdom and instruction.
Proverbs 1:7

Have you ever felt like your school work or homework was too hard? Or maybe your Sunday School teacher gives you too many Bible verses to memorize? Do you work hard and feel frustrated because it takes so long to get all the work done? Or do you write any sloppy thing down just to say you did the work, but you didn't learn anything from the assignment? Solomon taught that those who hate to learn new things are foolish, but showing respect and obedience to God is the first step in getting knowledge. Your respect and obedience to God gives you the right to ask Him to help you when you don't understand your school work or when the memory verses are long and hard to remember. Not only will God help you, but He will also put people that you trust in your life to help you when you don't understand.

Prayer: *Lord Jesus, some of my school subjects are not interesting, and I don't want to do the work. And some of my Bible verses are not only hard to understand, but also hard to memorize. I need your help to learn new things. Give me a hunger and desire to learn so that I can be well-educated in many subjects. Amen.*

Day #135   Dare To Be Different!

Take heed unto thyself, and unto the doctrine; continue in them: for in doing this thou shalt both save thyself, and them that hear thee.
1 Timothy 4:16

Do you have friends who do not live for the Lord like you do with all of their heart, mind, soul, and strength? Sometimes they may try to make you feel like you are not cool because of your Christian faith. Don't be intimidated! Dare to be different! Live for Jesus even if they make fun of you. Show them by your lifestyle that you have found the best way to live.[103] If you continue living in this way, Paul said that you will not only save yourself, but you will also save your friends who learn to believe by following the teachings that you share with them.

Prayer: *Lord Jesus, it is not always easy to go against the crowd, but I really do want to see my friends saved. Help me to dare to be different and share the love of Christ with my friends who haven't found you yet. Amen.*

---

[103] 2 Timothy 2:22.

Week 27 Review

Find the following words in the grid below.

Believers Charity Conversation Counsel Different Doctrine Example Faith Father Fool Friends Heaven Instruction Knowledge Light Obedience Parents Proverbs Purity Shine Solomon Teacher Wisdom World Youth

N	I	W	Z	O	B	E	D	I	E	N	C	E	I	U	X
R	J	Z	C	T	H	G	I	L	R	E	H	T	A	F	P
O	N	F	O	O	L	A	H	T	I	A	F	T	N	I	G
Z	M	I	U	W	N	O	I	Y	V	N	E	V	A	E	H
T	F	U	N	V	O	N	O	W	I	S	D	O	M	C	S
E	Q	D	S	S	I	U	D	I	F	F	E	R	E	N	T
A	J	M	E	S	T	T	E	N	I	R	T	C	O	D	P
C	I	P	L	H	A	R	P	G	W	O	R	L	D	I	S
H	E	G	A	W	S	I	U	R	D	F	F	S	R	R	O
E	L	P	V	R	R	X	P	C	O	E	D	V	E	X	L
R	P	U	Z	Q	E	O	N	Z	T	V	L	V	U	T	O
Y	M	R	S	W	V	N	R	D	O	I	E	W	P	I	M
K	A	I	H	C	N	K	T	Y	Y	I	O	R	O	N	O
M	X	T	I	F	O	N	J	S	L	D	R	N	B	N	N
Y	E	Y	N	D	C	C	H	E	M	W	J	Y	U	S	K
F	R	I	E	N	D	S	B	C	H	A	R	I	T	Y	R

Memory Verse: 1 Timothy 4:12 (Day #131)

Additional Memory Verse: Matthew 5:16 Day #132)

Week 28

God's Holy Children

But as he which hath called you is holy,
so be ye holy in all manner of conversation;
1 Peter 1:15

God's children are set apart unto Him.
Everything about their lifestyle shows their love and obedience to
Him.

David and Jonathan

Day #136   Chosen For Holiness

But ye are a chosen generation, a royal priesthood, an holy nation, a peculiar people; that ye should shew forth the praises of him who hath called you out of darkness into his marvellous light;
1 Peter 2:9[104]

From the time that Moses gave the Law to Israel until now, God has expected His chosen people to be separated from the world around them and live according to His wishes. The Israelites had very specific laws for worshiping, eating, dressing, decorating their homes, and arranging the crops in their fields. When a non-Jew saw an Israelite walking down the road, or if they passed an Israelite's home and field, there was no mistaking that they were God's people by the way they dressed and kept up their homes. Similarly, God still expects His New Testament chosen people to be recognized by their worship, appearance, conversation, and lifestyle.

Never be embarrassed about being different. Show the world your appreciation for being called out of sin's darkness into the bright and beautiful light of God's glory.

Prayer: *Lord Jesus, you are my heavenly Father and the Creator of everything. I want to live in such a way that people will see Christ in me and be drawn to that light to find a way out of the darkness of sin. Amen.*

Day #137   Holy To See God

Follow peace with all men, and holiness, without which no man shall see the Lord:
Hebrews 12:14

Jesus can give you peace of mind, because He is the Prince of Peace. Like Jesus, try to make peace everywhere you go. And be holy, like Jesus. Different from the world. Separate. Not ungodly like others in the world. Your Christ-like holiness will allow others to see Jesus in you. Your willingness to be different and obey God's laws will also give you the reward of seeing Him when your earthly life is over.

---

[104] See also Deuteronomy 7:6; 14:2; 22:5.

Prayer: *Lord Jesus, you paid for my sins with the blood you shed on Calvary, so you own me. I give myself to you to use me for your holy purpose. Let others see you living in me. I love you. Amen.*

Day #138 Relationships With Others

And be ye kind one to another, tenderhearted, forgiving one another, even as God for Christ's sake hath forgiven you.
Ephesians 4:32

Your holiness to God is tested by the way you treat others. Paul taught the Church at Ephesus to remember the way God forgave them when they were a sinner, so they could treat others the same way God had treated them. Kindness, tender hearts, and forgiving spirits toward others show Jesus how serious you are about living a holy lifestyle for Him.

Prayer: *Lord Jesus, I want to be holy like you. Guard my tongue, my heart and my attitude so that kindness, tenderness, and forgiveness will be formed in me and given freely to others. Amen.*

Day #139 Friendships

A man that hath friends must shew himself friendly: and there is a friend that sticketh closer than a brother.
Proverbs 18:24

The Bible tells a story of a prince named Jonathan who became friends with a poor shepherd boy named David. Jonathan could have chosen a friend who was wealthy like himself, but he chose David after he heroically killed the Philistine giant, Goliath. No doubt Jonathan also admired David's strong faith in God. Jonathan even shared some of his expensive, royal clothes and his weapons with David. They promised to be friends no matter what happened to them.[105] Although Jonathan was next in line to be the king of Israel, he was willing to step aside so that his best friend could become the next king. The best part of their friendship was that they both loved God and knew that He would be there for them when no one else would. If you want to have a friendship like Jonathan and

---

[105] 1 Samuel 18:1-4.

David, God's holy people will be willing to go out of their way to be friendly to someone else and get to know them.

Prayer: *Lord Jesus, sometimes I am shy around people I don't know very well. Help me to recognize those who aren't accepted by the crowd and give me the courage to be friendly to them and invite them to be a friend.*

Day #140 No Fake Love

*My little children, let us not love in word,
neither in tongue; but in deed and in truth.*
1 John 3:18

The Bible tells the story of King Saul who was jealous of David because he had killed Goliath and was popular with the people for his bravery.[106] Saul pretended to be David's friend and said David could marry his daughter if he would go and fight one hundred Philistines. But Saul was really hoping that David would get killed in the battle. The writer of 1 John tells us that we should not only tell someone we love them, but we should also prove our love by the nice things we say and do for them. Don't be like King Saul. God's holy people are not two-faced.

Prayer: *Lord Jesus, let my love for others be more than just talk. Help me to also show by my words and actions that I truly love them. Amen.*

---

[106] 1 Samuel 18:20-27.

Week 28 Review

Match the definitions on the left to the words on the right.

1. Chosen   ___ Forgiven

2. Royal   ___ Friendly

3. Holy   ___ Generation

4. Peculiar   ___ Goliath

5. Marvelous   ___ Holiness

6. No one sees God without this.   ___ Jonathan

7. Forgive and be ____.   ___ Light

8. Be kind and ____ to others.   ___ Nation

9. To have friends, you must be ____. ___ People

10. A friend of David.   ___ Priesthood

11. Philistine giant.   ___ Tenderhearted

12. Love others in deed and ____.   ___ Truth

Memory Verse: 1 Peter 2:9 (Day #136)

Additional Memory Verses: Hebrews 12:14 (Day #137); Ephesians 4:32 (Day #138); Proverbs 18:24 (Day #139); 1 John 3:18 (Day #140)

Week 29

7 Sins God Hates

The Boy Who Cried Wolf

Day #141   God Hates Sin

These six things doth the LORD hate:
yea, seven are an abomination unto him:
A proud look, a lying tongue, and hands that shed innocent blood,
An heart that deviseth wicked imaginations, feet that be swift
in running to mischief, A false witness that speaketh lies,
and he that soweth discord among brethren.
Proverbs 6:16-19

God has a very strong dislike or even hatred for people who are proud, those who tell lies on innocent people or kill them, those who think about doing evil things, those who tell lies in court, those who run around doing wrong things, and those who stir up trouble in their family. If you want God's hate to turn to love, then you must stop doing these wicked deeds and start obeying His commandments.[107]

Prayer: *Lord Jesus, forgive me when I sin against you. I want to obey your rules so that you will know that I truly do love you. Amen.*

Day #142   Pride Brings Destruction

Pride goeth before destruction, and an haughty spirit before a fall.
Proverbs 16:18

Several hundred years after the Israelites left Egypt, they decided they wanted a king like all the nations around them. God chose a fine young man named Saul to be the first king. He was shy and liked to tend to his own business. But after he became king, his position went to his head, and he became very proud. He made it known that he was the king, and nobody, including God or the prophet Samuel, could tell him what to do. After several years of ignoring God and the prophet, Samuel, God had enough of Saul's pride and disobedience. Samuel told Saul that God had rejected him from being king and had chosen another man who would be obedient to God's instructions. Saul knew the next king would be David,

---

[107] John 15:10

so he tried for several years to kill him. God protected David from Saul, and Saul ended up dying in battle at the hands of Israel's enemies.[108]

Pride will make you rebel against authority in your life, and you may eventually end up in jail or something worse.

Prayer: *Lord Jesus, thank you for putting parents, teachers, pastors, and other authority figures in my life. When I get mad at someone who tells me what to do, help me remember King Saul and the awful way his life ended because he refused to listen to advice from God and the prophet. Help me get pride out of my heart in Jesus' name. Amen.*

Day #143   Pride Brings You Down

A man's pride shall bring him low:
but honour shall uphold the humble in spirit.
Proverbs 29:23

People who are proud think they know more than others, and they will not listen to any other opinion but their own. They don't have many friends because they do not treat others kindly. Because they refuse to listen to instructions, they often find themselves in trouble with their parents and school teachers, and eventually, they become law-breakers.

On the other hand, those who have a kind and gentle attitude get special favors from the authority figures in their life. God notices their humility, and He honors them. People speak well of them because of their humility. The New Testament writers, James and Peter, stated that God resists or stands against those who are proud.[109] There is no chance of being truly successful in life if God is against you.

Prayer: *Lord Jesus, sometimes I feel like everyone is against me. I resent doing chores and spending time with my bratty brother or sister. If I fuss about being made to do things I don't want to do, I get grounded. I need a heart change. Forgive me for the pride in my heart and teach me to be kind, gentle, and obedient to those who are my authorities. In Jesus' name. Amen.*

---

[108] 1 Samuel 10, 13, 15, 31
[109] James 4:6; 1 Peter 5:5.

Day #144   God Hates Lying

Lying lips are abomination to the LORD:
but they that deal truly are his delight.
Proverbs 12:22[110]

The word *abomination* isn't commonly used in everyday language, so let's see how the dictionary defines it. An abomination is something shameful, strongly disliked, or even hated. God has a strong hatred for someone who tells lies, but He takes great delight in those who tell the truth. Do you want God to be delighted with you? Then always tell the truth.

Prayer: *Lord Jesus, when I am tempted to tell a lie to cover something I did wrong, help me remember that you delight in those who are truthful. Help me to tell the truth, even if I get in trouble. I want most of all, to please you. Amen.*

Day #145   Pray For Deliverance From Lying

Deliver my soul, O LORD, from lying lips, and from a deceitful tongue.
Psalms 120:2

Deceitful means to lie on purpose with the intention of persuading others to believe your lie. The little boy in the following story was a deceitful liar.

Long, long ago a man named Aesop[111] wrote a story about a little boy who was given a job to watch the sheep for the people in his town. His neighbors told him to shout really loud if the wolf came to attack the sheep, and they would immediately come and help him. Since the little boy was a chronic liar, he thought it would be fun to cry, "Wolf!" and make everyone come running. He did that several times when there was no wolf, and finally the neighbors decided to ignore the boy. One day the wolf did come, and all his cries brought him no help. The wolf destroyed every sheep in the flock, and the little boy learned the painful lesson that eventually no one will believe a liar, even when he is telling the truth.

Prayer: *Lord Jesus, let only true words come out of my lips. Amen.*

---

[110] More on Lying – Proverbs 12:19
[111] Aesop's Fables. *The Boy Who Cried Wolf.*

Week 29 Review

1. Circle the words or phrases which describe the 7 sins God hates. (Hint: There are more than 7.) Fill in the blanks for questions 2-9.

Silliness   Lying   Pride   Kicking the cat   Killing innocent people

Playing games   Evil thoughts   Troublemaker in the family

Eating broccoli   Running around doing wrong things   Singing

Tell lies in court   Hate the policeman   Read a magazine

2. Who was the first king of Israel? _____

3. Who does God stand against? _____

4. Who does God honor? _____

5. What does abomination mean? _____

_____

6. What is an abomination to the Lord? _____

7. Who does God delight in? _____

8. What lie did the little shepherd boy tell several times?

_____

9. What is the meaning of deceitful? _____

_____

Memory verse: Proverbs 16:18 (Day #142)

Additional Memory Verses: Proverbs 6:16-19 (Day #141)

Week 30

Things To Throw Away

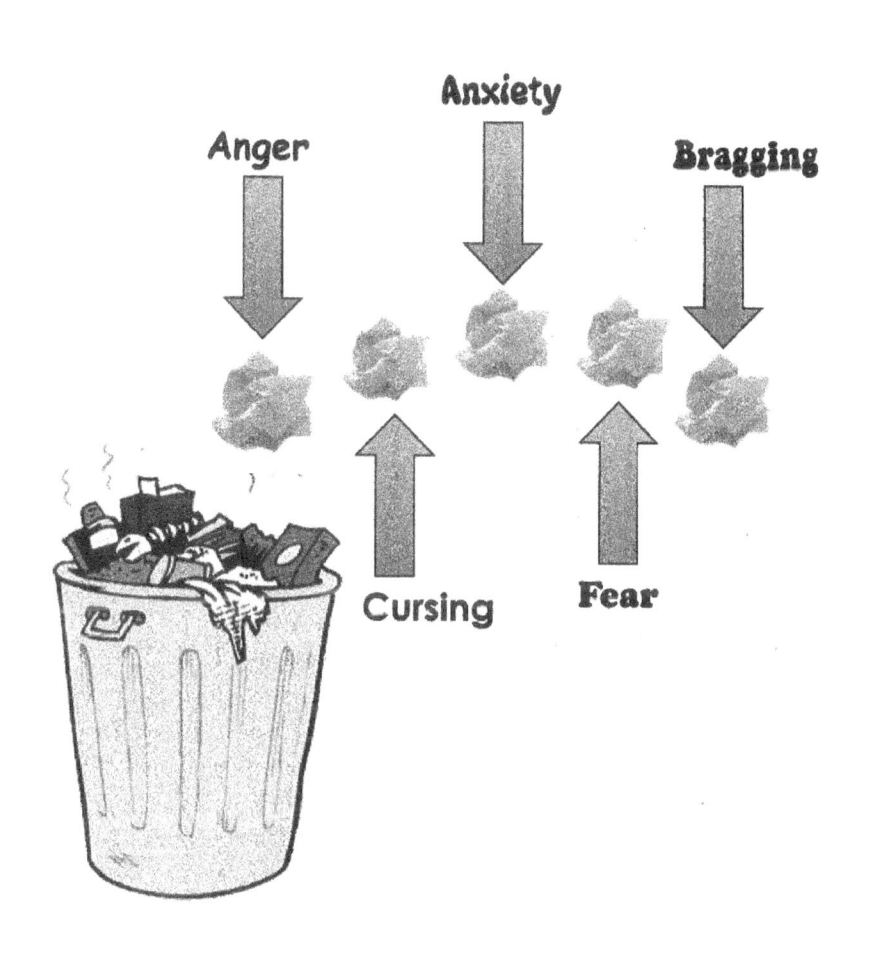

Day #146   Anger

A wrathful man stirreth up strife: but he that is slow to anger appeaseth strife.
Proverbs 15:18

The Bible tells a story of a man named Demetrius who was a silversmith in the city of Ephesus.[112] He made silver items for people to use in their worship of the false goddess Diana. He got very angry at the Apostle Paul one day because so many people were being converted to Christianity that few people were buying his silver creations. He got together with other silversmiths in the city, and their anger caused them to start a riot in the streets. People joined in, and for two hours mobs of people screamed, "Great is Diana of the Ephesians!" Finally, the town clerk was able to get their attention and calm everyone down and send them home. You can make the choice to be a Demetrius, whose anger stirs up an angry mob, or you can be like the town clerk who calmly breaks up the quarrel. The choice is yours.

Prayer: *Lord Jesus, when I am tempted to get angry and start a fuss, calm my spirit, and let me be a peacemaker instead.*

Day #147   Anxiety

*For God hath not given us the spirit of fear;
but of power, and of love, and of a sound mind.*
2 Timothy 1:7

Do thunderstorms, hurricanes, or tornadoes frighten you? I once lived in Iowa which was known for frequent tornados that came through that area at certain seasons of the year. We paid attention to weather forecasts and the storm sirens. But one night while my husband and I were conducting a Bible study in our home with several of our neighbors, a tornado ripped through the neighborhood and tore the roof off the house next to us. We were so focused on our lesson and discussion that we never heard the wind or the warning sirens. It wasn't until after the lesson was over and we walked outside that we learned of the storm damage to our neighbor's

---

[112] Acts 19:23-41

house. God had protected us during the storm, and He will protect you and keep you from being fearful of the weather.

Prayer: *Lord Jesus, I get very frightened when bad weather comes to my area. Help me to remember that you have promised me power, love, and a calm mind when storms come my way. Thank you for your promise.*

Day #148   Bragging

Let another man praise thee, and not thine own mouth;
a stranger, and not thine own lips.
Proverbs 27:2

Does it make you uncomfortable to be around someone who is always bragging about the things they have, the places they've been, or the good deeds they've done? Solomon said to keep silent about your skills and good deeds.

James agreed with Solomon's teaching when he said it is wrong to go around bragging about yourself.[113] You should wait for others to notice what you've done and praise you for it rather than bragging about yourself.

Prayer: *Lord Jesus, teach me to show humility when I do things well and let others praise my accomplishments.*

Day #149   Cursing

Thou shalt not take the name of the LORD thy God in vain;
for the LORD will not hold him guiltless that taketh his name in vain.
Exodus 20:7

God deserves our respect because He is our Creator, and He is holy. When we pray, He loves for us to call Him names like *Lord God* or *Lord Jesus*, but He is grieved when we use His name or title as a slang word. Sometimes people say, *"Oh my God"* when they are shocked, but this is disrespectful if you are not using this phrase in prayer. Some words like *gee, golly, gosh,* or

---

[113] James 4:16.

jeez are listed in the dictionary as slang words for Jesus or God. Be careful about using slang words that show disrespect for God or His name. Only speak His name or titles with respect and reverence.

Paul told the Ephesian Church members to stop talking dirty. The words that come out of your mouth should be appropriate for the situation and encourage others who need a word of cheer.[114]

Prayer: *Lord Jesus, forgive me when slang words slip out of my mouth. I really do want my words to honor you. Amen.*

Day #150   Fear

What time I am afraid, I will trust in thee. In God I will praise his word, in God I have put my trust; I will not fear what flesh can do unto me.
Psalms 56:3-4

So that we may boldly say, The Lord is my helper, and I will not fear what man shall do unto me.
Hebrews 13:6

Are you afraid of the dark? Does your stomach do flip-flops when all the lights go out, and you cover your head and can't sleep? Do you get fearful about taking a test at school or meeting new people? Always remember that God is with you, and He will take your fear away when you say the name, Jesus. Sometimes, a little song of praise to God can also help your fears to vanish. The little Veggie Tales characters sing this song, *"God is bigger than the boogie-man, and He's watching out for you and me."*[115]

Prayer: *Lord Jesus, your Word says that you are my helper, so when I start feeling fearful, I will put my trust for protection in you. Amen.*

---

[114] Don't speak filthy words. - Ephesians 4:29.
[115] Veggie-Tales; "Where's God When I'm S-Scared?" Big Idea Inc. 2008.

Week 30 Review

Complete the crossword below

Across
1. This emotion stirs up strife or conflict.
2. Do not take God's name in ___.
6. God is the ___ of all things.
8. Let another person ___ you.
9. You are ___ when you praise yourself.
10. God gives power, love and a sound ___.
11. Confidence in God to keep His promises.

Down
1. Fear of danger.
3. God has not given this spirit to you.
4. A silversmith from Ephesus.
5. Trust in God when you are ___.
7. The goddess of Ephesus in Paul's day.

Memory verse: 2 Timothy 1:7 (Day #147)

Additional Memory Verses: Psalms 56:3-4 (Day #150)

Week 31

More Things To Toss

Gossip Jealousy Laziness PANIC Wrath

Day #151   Gossip

Where no wood is, there the fire goeth out:
so where there is no talebearer, the strife ceaseth.
Proverbs 26:20

Tattletales! Gossipers! Those who spread rumors! There is a story from the Veggie Tales Collection called *Larry-Boy and the Rumor Weed*. In this story, two children discuss whether a respected man in the town is really a scary robot. A weed hears their words and begins spreading false rumors about this man all over town. Every time the rumors got passed to someone else, more untruths were added to the story about this man. The rumors were finally stopped when the children made a public announcement that Mr. Alfred was really a nice man who came to their school and told stories to their class.[116]

The wise King Solomon teaches that those who are tattletales start fires with their gossip, and those fires continue to spread until someone decides to stop the rumors. He also said that those who keep their mouths shut will stay out of trouble.[117] Don't be the talebearer who starts fires; instead, be the person who stops the fire with kind words or no words.

Prayer: *Lord Jesus, people can be hurt when others spread rumors about them. Help me to think before I speak and pray about things that concern me about others rather than spreading rumors about them. Amen.*

Day #152   Jealousy

Rejoice with them that do rejoice, and weep with them that weep.
Romans 12:15

Have you ever been resentful when one of your friends gets a new game or a certain brand of shoes that you had been wanting for a long time? It is human nature to be jealous when good things happen to other people instead of you, and it is easy to say, "I told you so," when something bad happens to them. But Paul said to be happy for others when good things

---

[116] Veggie Tales, Larry-Boy and the Rumor Weed; Big Idea Productions, Inc. 1999.
[117] Proverbs 21:23.

happen to them, and to feel true sorrow for them when something hurtful takes place.

Prayer: *Lord Jesus, help me to think less about my wishes and problems. I want to be happy when good things happen to my friends and feel sorrow for them when they are hurting.*

Day #153   Laziness

*He also that is slothful in his work
is brother to him that is a great waster.*
Proverbs 18:9[118]

The wise King Solomon taught us that lazy people are wasteful people. They waste time wishing they had the things their hard-working friends have, but they are too lazy to work for them. Has your mother ever said, "I want you to clean your room right now," but you were reading a book or playing a video game, so your response was, "Just five more minutes"? Soon five minutes turns into ten minutes, ten minutes turns into twenty, and you can never get the wasted time back.

Paul also condemned laziness. He said if someone was too lazy to work, then they should not expect hard-working people to give them food.[119] How many times do more appealing activities steal your time from God and your daily chores? God blesses those who work hard and do their very best in their school work, their work at home, and their work for God.

Prayer: *Lord Jesus, I know you want me to work hard, but sometimes I don't like cleaning my room or doing boring school work. It is more fun to play. Help me to learn the importance of hard work and to understand that if I don't work, I won't get paid, and if I don't do my school work, I won't get promoted to the next grade in school, and if I don't obey the Bible, I won't get to spend eternity in Heaven with you. Amen.*

---

[118] Proverbs 21:25.
[119] 2 Thessalonians 3:10-12.

Day #154   Panic

Fear thou not; for I am with thee: be not dismayed; for I am thy God:
I will strengthen thee; yea, I will help thee; yea,
I will uphold thee with the right hand of my righteousness.
Isaiah 41:10

Have you ever been separated from your parents while shopping in a large store? Often when we find ourselves alone, we may panic or become very frightened. John the Baptist and Jesus spent time alone in the wilderness before they began their public ministry. Saul's jealousy caused him to chase David away from his home, and David spent much time alone in caves and hiding places. He wrote about many of his experiences in the book of Psalms. Most importantly, he learned that God was always with him, and during his times of being alone, He could talk to God in prayer, for God is a very good listener.

Prayer: *Lord Jesus, thank you for the promise that you are always with me, and when I am afraid, you will calm me and give me the strength I need to get rid of my fear. I love you! Amen.*

Day #155   Wrath

A soft answer turneth away wrath: but grievous words stir up anger.
Proverbs 15:1

Make no friendship with an angry man; and with a furious man thou shalt not go:
Lest thou learn his ways, and get a snare to thy soul.
Proverbs 22:24-25

Have you ever noticed that when two people start arguing, their voices get louder and louder as they continue fighting? Sometimes the voices of parents or other adults cannot be heard because of the loud arguing. The Bible teaches that you shouldn't make friends with someone who has an anger problem because you will become like them and stir up anger everywhere you go. If you do get angry on occasion, make sure you apologize quickly.[120] Then, the next time someone tries to start an argument with you, try using soft, kind words to put an end to it.

Prayer: *Lord Jesus, help me to choose my friends carefully and stay calm, and speak softly and kindly when someone tries to start an argument with me. Amen.*

---

[120] Ephesians 4:26 – *Be ye angry, and sin not: let not the sun go down upon your wrath.*

Week 31 Review

Complete the crossword below

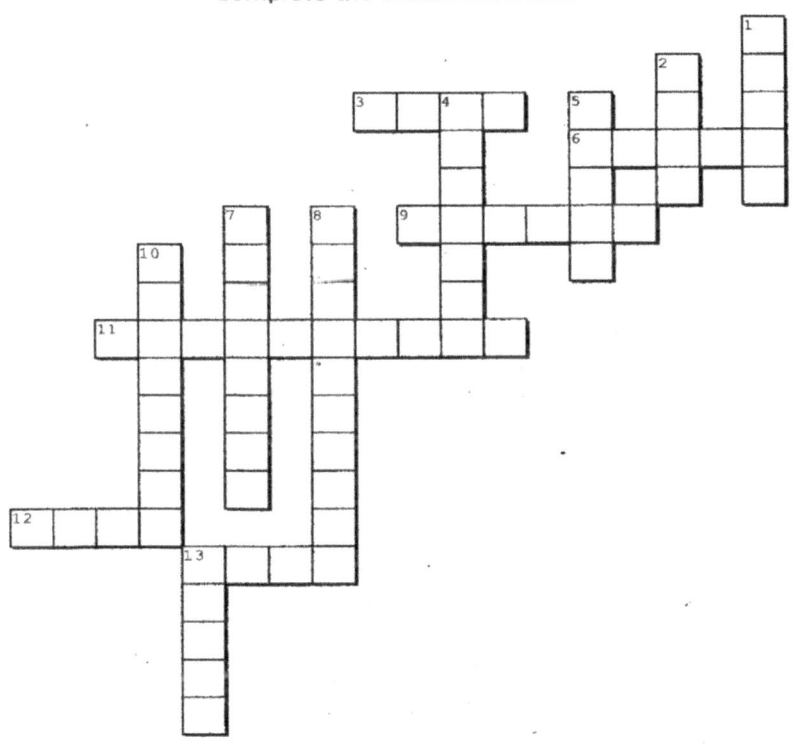

Across
3. God blesses those who ___ hard.
6. David spent much time ___ with his sheep.
9. Tattletales start fires with their ___.
11. Without a ___, strife ceases.
12. ___ people are wasteful people.
13. Tears shed when others are hurting.

Down
1. Grievous words stir up ___.
2. Without ___, a fire goes out.
4. Be glad when good things happen to others.
5. Sudden fear for no reason.
7. God promises to give ___ to those who are fearful.
8. Make no ___ with an angry man.
10. Resentment when someone has something you want.
13. A soft answer turns away ___.

Memory verse: Proverbs 15:1 (Day #155)

Additional Memory Verses: Ephesians 4:26 – *Be ye angry, and sin not: let not the sun go down upon your wrath.*

Week 32

My Body - God's Temple

Sleep Well

Day #156   Your Body Belongs To God

What? know ye not that your body is the temple of the Holy Ghost which is in you, which ye have of God, and ye are not your own? For ye are bought with a price: therefore glorify God in your body, and in your spirit, which are God's.
1 Corinthians 6:19-20[121]

Paul taught the Corinthian believers that Jesus had paid for their body by His death on the cross, so that gave Him exclusive ownership to the bodies of His believers. Because you are a Christian, you do not represent yourself when you are around other people. You represent Jesus, and your appearance and attitude should bring glory to your owner.

Prayer: *Lord Jesus, I didn't realize that my behavior and my appearance at home and in public will either honor you or disgrace you. I would never want to bring disgrace to you. Forgive me for the times I have dressed sloppily or had a bad attitude around others. Let me be a shining light in a very dark world. Amen.*

Day #157   Your Body Is God's Temple

Know ye not that ye are the temple of God, and that the Spirit of God dwelleth in you? If any man defile the temple of God, him shall God destroy; for the temple of God is holy, which temple ye are.
1 Corinthians 3:16-17

Paul reminded the Corinthian believers again that their bodies were God's Temple, and God would not tolerate anyone mistreating their body. Your body is holy, and when you destroy its beauty either inside or outside by making unwise choices, God's Temple is dishonored. Paul said punishment awaits those who dishonor God's Temple. So, take care of your body for your owner.

Prayer: *Lord Jesus, I am learning so much about how to please you with the choices I make each day concerning my body. I understand now that I belong to you, and I want my body to bring honor to you every day. Amen.*

---

[121] See also: Romans 12:1-2.

Day #158   Live Life In Balance

For bodily exercise profiteth little: but godliness is profitable unto all things, having promise of the life that now is, and of that which is to come.
1 Timothy 4:8

Exercise is a key part of living a healthy life, but Paul's teaching was not only about exercise. He wanted young Timothy to keep balance in his life. You can't spend an hour a day at the gym, but neglect to study your Bible, pray, or attend church. Paul said that a Godly lifestyle would benefit you in every area of your life both now and in the life to come, so your spiritual habits need to have a higher priority than your health habits. For example, maybe your morning routine involves running a mile, then doing your devotions while you cool down; but one day you wake up late and don't have time for both. Then the Bible devotions would take priority over the running. The main point is to stay balanced, but always keep God first.

Prayer: *Lord Jesus, I want to be healthy in body, soul, and spirit. Help me to keep the right balance in every area of my life. Amen.*

Day #159   You Need Your Rest

It is vain for you to rise up early, to sit up late, to eat the bread of sorrows: for so he giveth his beloved sleep.
Psalms 127:2

Before electricity was invented, people went to bed when it got dark outside, and they woke up when it got light, but electricity in our homes has changed the sleep patterns of most people. However, the Bible teaching on getting enough sleep to be healthy has not changed. The Psalmist said you should not get up early and stay up late to worry about all your problems because God has provided sleep so His beloved people can rest. When your parents say it is bedtime, trust them to know what is best for your health. Get your rest at night, and do your best to get your work and play done during the day.

Prayer: *Lord Jesus, I want to be healthy and get the right amount of rest each day. I'm thankful that my parents have a set time for me to go to bed each night and a time to wake up. Thank you for the gift of rest after a hard day's work. Amen.*

Day #160   Don't Sleep Too Much

Love not sleep, lest thou come to poverty;
open thine eyes, and thou shalt be satisfied with bread.
Proverbs 20:13

The Bible teaches you that getting the right amount of rest is important to your health, but if you spend too much time in bed, much valuable time that could be spent in doing productive work is forever lost. Has your mom ever come into your room to wake you up for school or Church, and you just lie there thinking you want a few more minutes to sleep? Then when you finally get up, you find yourself rushing to get ready and eat so you won't be late. Staying in bed after you should be up doesn't give you more rest; instead, it creates more stress. Learn how much sleep you need in order to spend your awake time doing your work and enjoying fun times with family and friends.

Prayer: *Lord Jesus, I don't want to be poor and hungry because I sleep too much to work for the things I need. Help me to rest well when I'm in bed and be thankful for the good health you give me so I can work hard and enjoy times of fun when I am awake.*

Week 32 Review

Use the word list to fill in the blanks of the sentences below.

activities - attitude – balance - body – care – cross – Exercise - glory – health - healthy - holy – laziness - mistreat – neglect - owner – posture – problem - rest - sins – sleep - spirit – Temple – work - worrying.

God is the _____ of your _____ because He paid for your _____ when He died on the _____. Your appearance and your _____ should bring _____ to your owner. Your body is _____ because it is God's _____. Don't _____ your body. Take very good _____ of it for your owner. _____ helps keep your physical body _____, and Bible study and other spiritual _____ keep your _____ healthy. Don't _____ exercise for the body or spirit. Keep your life in _____. God gives _____ to His children to give their bodies a _____. Don't stay up too late _____ about your math test or some other _____ in your life. God's Temple needs the right amount of sleep to maintain good _____. Although sleep is necessary for good health, too much sleep can promote _____ and prevent you from getting all your _____ done.

Memory verse: <u>Psalms 127:2</u> (Day #159)
Additional Memory Verses: <u>1 Corinthians 6:19-20</u> (Day #156)

Week 33

Miracles For Children

Jairus' daughter raised from the dead

Day #161   Boy From Zarephath

And Elijah took the child, and brought him down out of the chamber into the house, and delivered him unto his mother: and Elijah said, See, thy son liveth. And the woman said to Elijah, Now by this I know that thou art a man of God, and that the word of the LORD in thy mouth is truth.
1 Kings 17:23-24

During a famine in Israel because there had been no rain, Elijah left the country and found a place to stay with a widow and her son. Throughout the famine, the widow's container of meal and oil continued to multiply just enough each day to feed the three of them. One day, the widow's son got very sick and died. She was so grieved to lose her only son. Elijah was also grieved, but he took the boy upstairs to the room where he was staying and laid him on the bed. Three times Elijah prayed and asked God to restore the boy. On the third time, the boy revived, and Elijah brought him back down to his mother.[122] She was more convinced than ever after that miracle that Elijah was a man of God.

In her time of crisis, the widow had a trusted prophet to call on to pray for her son. Everyone has times of difficulty in their lives. During those times, you need a pastor in your life; not one that you watch on the internet or television. You need one who knows your family and can pray for you and give guidance during the hard times in your life.

Prayer: *Lord Jesus, I am thankful that you have given pastors to feed and minister to your people when they have problems. Thank you for my pastor who loves me and prays for me. Amen.*

---

[122] 1 Kings 17:8-24.

Day #162   Boy From Shunem

And she went up, and laid [her son] on the bed of the man of God, and shut the door upon him, and went out. Then she saddled an ass, and said to her servant, Drive, and go forward; slack not thy riding for me, except I bid thee. So she went and came unto the man of God to mount Carmel…
2 Kings 4:21, 24-25

The Bible tells a story of a great woman who lived in Shunem with her husband. They got acquainted with the prophet Elisha and wanted to do something special for him. So, they built an extra room onto their home and furnished it for him to use any time he was passing through their town. The couple didn't have any children, so Elisha prophesied that they would soon have a son. No doubt there was excitement in the house the day that little boy was born. But one day when the boy was older, he was in the field with his dad, and he started complaining about his head. A servant carried him home to his mother, and he died shortly afterward. This great woman took her son to the prophet's room and laid him on the bed. Then she got on a donkey and rode to where Elisha was staying at the time. When Elisha asked how everyone was, this great lady made a statement of faith by saying everything was well. Elisha could tell something terrible had happened, so he and Gehazi went back to her house where they found the dead child on his bed. Elisha shut the door and prayed two times. Soon the boy began sneezing and opened his eyes. He called the mother into the room and gave her son back to her.[123]

What if the parents had not made a room for the prophet years before their son died? Who would they have called in their time of grief? You need a pastor in your life. Pray for him and do special things for him because there will surely come a day when you need prayer from the pastor who loves you.

Prayer: Lord Jesus, I see how important it is to have a pastor who knows my family and can be called upon when we have a desperate need. Amen

---

[123] 2 Kings 4:8-37.

Day #163   Boy From Nain

Now when he came nigh to the gate of the city, behold, there was a dead man carried out, the only son of his mother, and she was a widow: and much people of the city was with her. And when the Lord saw her, he had compassion on her, and said unto her, Weep not.
Luke 7:12-13

One day Jesus and His disciples visited the city of Nain. As he neared the city gate, he noticed the funeral procession of a young boy being carried to his grave. His mother had lost her husband to death, and now her only son had also died. Jesus had compassion on the mother and told her not to cry. Then, He stopped the funeral procession and told the boy to arise. Immediately, the boy sat up and began to talk. He got down off the stretcher where he had been lying and returned to his mother. That miracle was the talk of the town for a long time.[124] Wonderful things happen when Jesus comes to town.

Prayer: *Lord Jesus, you really do care when people are hurting. Because you are so kind to people when they have a need, I know I can trust you with all my secrets and tell you when my heart is hurting. Thank you that you are my comforter. Amen.*

Day #164   Jairus' Daughter

And, behold, there came a man named Jairus, and he was a ruler of the synagogue: and he fell down at Jesus' feet, and besought him that he would come into his house: For he had one only daughter, about twelve years of age, and she lay a dying. But as he went the people thronged him.
Luke 8:41-42

Jairus was a leader in the church, and his only daughter, who was twelve years old, got very sick. He found Jesus and asked Him to come and heal her, but on the way to his house, another lady needed healing. By the time they finally arrived, the daughter had already died. Jesus told Jairus not to be afraid, but to believe, and she would be well. He took only three of His disciples and the girl's parents into the room with Him. He took her by the

---

[124] Luke 7:11-17.

hand and told her to wake up, and she did.[125] Some of the people at Jairus' house thought Jesus had arrived too late, but Jesus is never late. Instead of healing a very sick girl, He was able to perform a greater miracle by raising her from the dead.

When your prayers don't get answered the way you think they should, just wait and believe. Jesus will answer in His time, and you will be glad you waited.

Prayer: *Lord Jesus, it is hard for me to wait for something I really want. But I see from this story that waiting gave the family a greater blessing than if you had come when they first asked you. Forgive me for my impatience, and teach me Lord, to wait Amen.*

Day #165   Eutychus From Troas

And there sat in a window a certain young man named Eutychus, being fallen into a deep sleep: and as Paul was long preaching, he sunk down with sleep, and fell down from the third loft, and was taken up dead.
Acts 20:9

During one of Paul's missionary journeys, he spent a week in the city of Troas. On the night before he was to leave, the church members met on the third floor of a building and listened to Paul preach one last time. The windows were open, and a young boy named Eutychus was sitting in the window. Paul preached till midnight, and the boy fell asleep and fell out of the third story window all the way to the ground. He died instantly. Paul went outside and picked up the boy and said he was going to be all right. So, everyone went back inside the house, ate some food, and continued the meeting until the sun came up. Eutychus was totally well, and everyone was comforted that God had worked a miracle for them.[126]

No doubt there were Church members who chose not to attend service that night. Can you imagine how they felt about missing out on all the excitement? You never know what kind of surprises and blessings God has in store for those who come to Church. Don't miss Church.

---

[125] Matthew 9:18-26; Mark 5:22-43; Luke 8:41-56.
[126] Acts 20:7-12.

Prayer: *Lord Jesus, sometimes I get sleepy in church just like Eutychus did, and I'd rather be home in my bed. But Eutychus experienced a miracle that night that forever changed his life. He probably never missed a church service after that. Help me to be excited about going to church every time it is scheduled. I don't want to miss a thing that you have for me to receive. Amen.*

Week 33 Review

Match the definitions on the left to the words on the right.

1. Elijah stayed here during a famine.   ____. Built room.

2. What happened to the meal and oil?   ____ Eutychus

3. What miracle did the widow receive?   ____ Gehazi

4. Elisha's prophecy to Shunamite lady.   ____ Jairus

5. Favor for Elisha from Shunamite couple.   ____ Midnight

6. Elisha's servant.   ____ Multiplied

7. Jesus resurrected a boy from ____.   ____ Twelve

8. Boy's mother was a ____.   ____ Son was born

9. Ruler of the synagogue.   ____ Son resurrected

10. Age of Jairus' daughter.   ____ Nain

11. How late did Paul preach?   ____ Widow

12. He fell out of the upstairs window.   ____ Zarephath

Memory verse: Matthew 7:7-8 - *Ask, and it shall be given you; seek, and ye shall find, knock, and it shall be opened unto you: - For every one that asketh receiveth; and he that seeketh findeth; and to him that knocketh it shall be opened.*

Additional Memory Work: Ephesians 6:13-17.
Learn the 6 pieces of the Armor of God.
1) Belt of Truth
2) Breastplate of Righteousness
3) Shoes of Peace
4) Shield of Faith
5) Helmet of Salvation
6) Sword of the Spirit

Week 34

Modern Day Heroes

Ashley and Dusty

Day #166   Hubert Rescues Linda

Beloved, if God so loved us, we ought also to love one another.
1 John 4:11

On a chilly January 25th in Indian Village, LA, 8-year-old Hubert was sitting by the fireplace with his little sister, Linda, who had turned 1-year-old that day. She was rocking in a little chair with her back to the fire. Suddenly, she rocked too hard, and the chair turned over backwards, throwing Linda head first into the fire. Hubert jumped up and pulled her out of the fireplace, but her hair was on fire. He grabbed a nearby blanket, wrapped her head up, and ran outside where he was able to put out the fire and save her life. Their parents didn't take her to a hospital because they lived so far out of town. Instead, their mother, Hattie, sent one of the older brothers to get a neighbor, affectionately called Mamaw, to come and pray for Linda. Hattie took care of the burns on Linda's head and back until they were healed. It was a long time before she could lie on her back, and the hair never grew back on the back part of her head that was burned. Hubert's love for his baby sister and quick action saved her life. Hubert grew up to be a Godly husband and father of five children. Little sister, Linda, grew up and married a Pentecostal preacher named Carroll, and they had three children. Their ministry has affected Churches all over North America as they have preached and sung wherever they were invited to minister.[127] When you let God use you to help others like young Hubert did, God will continue to guide your life according to His plan.

Prayer: *Lord Jesus, sometimes I don't feel very special, but here I am, available for you to use my life to be a blessing to someone else. Amen.*

---

[127] Story as told to Pam Eddings by her dad, Hubert Nixon and his sister, Linda Bushnell on October 12, 2015.

Day #167   Clifford Helps Oliver

A friend loveth at all times, and a brother is born for adversity.
Proverbs 17:17

True friends will be there for you in good times and bad. They love you when you're happy, and they love you when you're sad. But brothers and sisters are given to you so that in the tough times of life, you have someone who loves you to stand beside you and help you get through your problems.

Oliver and Clifford were the older brothers of the nine children in the Hale family. One summer when Oliver was about ten years old, he and his younger brother, Clifford, were helping their dad get the tomato crop harvested so they could take them to the canning factory. They had piled a load of tomatoes on their old truck, and as they were climbing a hill past the house, the truck stalled and started to slide backward. Oliver quickly jumped out and found a rock to slip under the wheel, but he slipped in the loose gravel and fell under the truck. The truck rolled backward over his arm and both legs before his dad was able to get it stopped. Clifford quickly ran home to tell their mom who was picking more tomatoes for the next load. When she saw the frightened look on Clifford's face, she feared the worst, and came running out to the road. Mr. Hale gently carried Oliver home, and he and his wife prayed for him. Mrs. Hale checked to make sure there were no broken bones, and she gave him constant care. Oliver was in bed for over a month before he could walk again. During that time, his younger brother, Clifford, willingly worked longer hours so that he could do both his and his brother's work while Oliver recovered.[128] That is the kind of brother that the above verse was talking about. If you have a brother, sister, or friend to help in times of trouble, you are blessed.

Prayer: *Lord Jesus, I thank you for my friends and family. Sometimes we don't get along with each other, but it is comforting to remember that when times get tough, true friends and family will always be there for me.*

---

[128] Imagene Eddings, *"In The Attic"* (Springfield, MO: Gospel Publishing House, 1995) pgs. 39-40. [Note: Oliver and Clifford were the older brothers of Imagene Hale Eddings.]

Day #168   Ashley Protects Dusty

*Therefore will not we fear, though the earth be removed,
and though the mountains be carried into the midst of the sea;*
Psalms 46:2

When Ashley was eight years old, an F5 tornado hit Wichita, Kansas on April 26, 1991. On that day, the family suddenly heard a sound like the rumbling of a train heading down the street. Ashley's dad told everyone in the house to quickly take cover, so Ashley, her brother Dusty, the baby sitter, her three kids, and Ashley's dad all rushed to the living room closet to take shelter. Ashley and Dusty were crouched closest to the door, and at the last moment before the tornado hit, Ashley shoved her brother beneath her to protect him. After the deafening roar of the tornado had passed, Ashley's dad shoved the closet door open, which was blocked by the couch. When everyone stepped out of the closet, the house they were in had been totally destroyed. The only four walls left standing were the closet walls where they had hidden. At first no one moved as they looked in awe at the devastation around them. Then, they began inspecting the house. Ashley walked back into the closet and noticed that on the right inside wall of the closet where Dusty had first stood, a large piece of glass had penetrated the wall. If she had not shoved him beneath her, that piece of glass would have hit him in the head. She said she did not know what made her cover him at the last minute, but she was so glad that she did.[129]

It is a normal feeling to be afraid of storms, but the Psalmist reminds us that even when the earth is shaking all around us, we can trust the Lord and not let fear overcome us. Just call the name of Jesus during your storm, and He will protect you.

Prayer: *Lord Jesus, when storms come, I want to be close to my parents or someone older who can protect me, but I'm thankful to know that you are always near and ready to help when I cry out to you. Amen.*

---

[129] This story was told to me by my daughter-in-law, Ashley Eddings on October 15, 2015.

Day #169   Virgil Saves Jared From Drowning

> *But now thus saith the LORD that created thee… Fear not: for I have redeemed thee, I have called thee by thy name; thou art mine. When thou passest through the waters, I will be with thee; and through the rivers, they shall not overflow thee: when thou walkest through the fire, thou shalt not be burned; neither shall the flame kindle upon thee.*
> Isaiah 43:1-2

One summer day Arleta and her sister, Margo, and brother-in-law, Virgil decided to take their families to the creek to swim. There were seven children between the two families. For a while everyone was having a good time floating and splashing in the shallow water near the bank. Arleta's son, Jared, had not yet learned how to swim, and he suddenly found himself in water too deep to touch the bottom. He disappeared from sight. Meanwhile Jared's Uncle Virgil, who had been keeping a close watch on all the children to make sure they were safe, suddenly realized there were only six children in the water. As he was trying to figure out which one was missing, he suddenly saw some hair sticking up out of the water. He quickly reached out and grabbed the hair and discovered it was his nephew, Jared. Uncle Virgil's quick action saved Jared from drowning that day![130]

Psalms 91:11-12 reminds us that God puts angels in charge of watching over his children. No doubt Arleta's prayers for her children before they ever left home had caused God to dispatch an angel to protect him from downing.

Prayer: *Lord Jesus, thank you for your promise to send an angel to protect me when I get into trouble while swimming or playing around a camp fire. Amen.*

---

[130] This story was told to me by my daughter-in-law, Desiree Eddings on October 16, 2015. Desiree is Arleta's daughter and Jared's sister. Virgil and Margo are Desiree's uncle and aunt.

Day #170   Allan Tries Until He Succeeds

I can do all things through Christ which strengtheneth me.
Philippians 4:13

Allan Oggs was born with cerebral palsy.[131] His parents never told him that he was handicapped. Even though doctors had said Allan would never walk, talk, or do things that other children did, Allan's parents kept praying for him and teaching him that he could do anything he wanted to do. He had to work much harder than other children to learn to crawl, walk, feed himself, and dress himself, but he had a strong will to do things without help, and he amazed the doctors with all of his achievements. He even taught himself to ride a bike after many falls over several days. He attended regular classes all through his school years. His dad was a Pentecostal preacher, and after a period of wandering around trying to decide what to do with his life, Allan surrendered his life to God and was called to preach. He attended Bible school, got married, and he and his wife had three children. He became known all over the United States and even appeared on Dr. Dobson's *Focus on the Family* broadcast. He wrote a book titled, *You've Got To Have The Want To.* No matter what type of handicaps you may have, you can accomplish your dreams through prayer and strong desire.

Prayer: *Lord Jesus, I don't like to be laughed at when I can't do something as well as other boys and girls my age. Help me remember that you will help me overcome any obstacle that I face so that I can succeed in life. Amen.*

---

[131] Cerebral palsy is an injury to the brain that affects how certain muscles of the body are able to function.

Week 34 Review

Answer True or False for each statement below.

____1. Because God loves us, we don't have to love each other.

____2. Hubert saved his little sister from the fire.

____3. Friends love you all the time.

____4. Brothers are there for you when you have a problem.

____5. Oliver was run over by a train.

____6. If the mountains fall into the sea, I will be afraid.

____7. Ashley and Dusty were alone in a closet when a tornado hit.

____8. God promises protection in water and fire.

____9. Jared was saved from drowning by his Uncle Virgil.

____10. Angels watch over God's children.

____11. God only gives strength to do certain things.

____12. Allan overcame cerebral palsy and became a preacher.

Memory verse: Philippians 4:13 (Day #170)

Additional Memory Verses: 1 John 4:11 (Day #166); Proverbs 17:17 (Day #167)

Week 35

If You Will, God Will

The word IF is a tiny two-letter conjunction that appears in the King James Version of the Bible 1,595 times. In dozens of cases, IF is used to begin a statement that has conditions attached. For example, IF you clean your room, I will let you invite a friend over to play. God is a God of love and mercy, but often He attaches conditions to receiving blessings from Him. This week we will look at just a few IF statements between God and people.

Peter wept after denying that he knew Jesus

Day #171 God Forgives IF You Confess

IF we confess our sins, he is faithful and just to forgive us our sins, and to cleanse us from all unrighteousness.
1 John 1:9

Manasseh became king of Israel when he was twelve years old, and he ruled for fifty-five years. From the beginning of his reign, he rebelled against the God of Israel. He became worse with each year. When he was older, he set up altars and idols to false gods in the holy Temple of the true God. He even sacrificed his children on the fiery altars of false gods. Prophets tried to warn him to turn from his sins, but he ignored all of them. Finally, God had no choice but to allow the Assyrian armies to capture him and bring him bound to Babylon. The time in prison finally got his attention, and he repented and sought God's forgiveness for the horrible things he had done. God heard his prayer and allowed him to get released and return to his throne in Jerusalem. For the rest of his life, he served God and encouraged the people of Judah to serve God also.[132]

God promises punishment IF His laws are not obeyed; but IF a person repents, God forgives and removes the sin from their record. So, always remember: IF you sin, God will forgive, IF you repent.

Prayer: *Lord Jesus, sometimes when I do something wrong, a little voice in my head tells me it is no use to say I'm sorry because you are mad at me and don't want to hear from me. But I am thankful for Manasseh's story and the verse for today which reminds me that you will forgive IF I will confess my sin to you. Amen.*

Day #172 God Keeps His Promises IF You Obey

The Lord is not slack concerning his promise, as some men count slackness; but is longsuffering to us-ward, not willing that any should perish, but that all should come to repentance.
2 Peter 3:9

---

[132] You can read Manasseh's story in 2 Kings 21 and 2 Chronicles 33.

The night that Jesus was arrested by soldiers, all His disciples fled except for John. Later, Peter followed the soldiers to learn what would happen to Jesus. Three times someone recognized him as a follower of Jesus, and because he was afraid of getting arrested, he said he didn't know Jesus. On the third time, a rooster crowed, and Jesus turned and looked at Peter. Peter remembered that Jesus had warned him about denying Him, and he went out and cried a long time.[133]

After Jesus was resurrected, He met Peter privately and during their conversation, Peter repented, and Jesus gave him the job of feeding His sheep, which means to teach the people about Jesus.[134] When Peter wrote his second letter to the Church, he could say from experience that God really does keep His promises, IF a person obeys His Word.

Prayer: *Lord Jesus, I thank you for your mercy and your willingness to forgive my sins against you and others, IF I am truly sorry and ask for forgiveness.*

Day #173   God Keeps Loving IF You Keep Obeying

*IF ye keep my commandments, ye shall abide in my love;
even as I have kept my Father's commandments, and abide in his love.*
John 15:10

God is serious about His laws. He loves all of His children, but on two occasions in the book of John, He makes one of His IF statements about love and obedience. In the first statement, He says IF you love Him, you'll obey Him,[135] and in the verse for today, He says, IF you obey Him, He will keep on loving you. Love and obedience are tied together so that one cannot be separated from the other. God will keep on loving you, IF you keep on obeying His Word.

Prayer: *Lord Jesus, no one ever loved me like you do. I don't ever want to displease you by rebelling against your commandments. I want to love and obey you for the rest of my life. Amen.*

---

[133] Mt. 26:34-75; Mk 14:29-31, 53-72; Lk 22:31-34, 54-62; Jn 13:37-38
[134] Jn. 21:15-17.
[135] John 14:15.

Day #174   God Will Lead You IF You Trust Him

Trust in the LORD with all thine heart; and lean not unto thine own understanding. In all thy ways acknowledge him, and he shall direct thy paths.
Proverbs 3:5-6

King Zedekiah was the last king of Judah. During his reign, King Nebuchadnezzar of Babylon sent his army to Jerusalem to capture the king and take thousands of Israelites as prisoners and bring them back to Babylon. Treasures of gold, silver, and precious furniture were stolen from the beautiful Temple and brought to King Nebuchadnezzar. Then the Temple and the city of Jerusalem were burned.[136]

Seventy years later King Artaxerxes told Ezra that he could take anyone back to Israel who wanted to go. Over 1,700 people volunteered to go back home. The trip was very dangerous because many thieves would hide out along the roads and rob anyone who came by. Since the Israelites didn't have an army escort to keep them safe, they fasted and prayed for three days before leaving Babylon and asked God to protect them. The king also gave them money and returned all of the Temple treasures that had been stolen so they could bring them back to Jerusalem. Ezra divided the treasures between twelve trusted men and made them promise to guard the treasures and keep them safe until they arrived in Jerusalem. God protected the entire group from robbers and brought them all safely back to Jerusalem. The twelve men also gave all the Temple treasures to the priests after their arrival in the city.[137]

Ezra had selected twelve men to trust with God's treasures, and they did not disappoint him by being careless with the valuables in their possession. We all have people in our life that we trust with our secrets and our prayer needs, but do we trust God? Trusting in the Lord is mentioned over sixty times in the Bible. He is trustworthy and will never betray your secrets. IF you trust Him, He will lead you in the direction you need to go.

---

[136] 2 Kings 25.
[137] Ezra 8.

Prayer: *Lord Jesus, forgive me when I put my trust in people more than I trust in you. I do want you to direct my life in the way that you have planned for me. Help me to trust you more. Amen.*

Day #175   Desires Granted IF You Delight In God

***Delight** thyself also in the LORD: and he shall give thee the desires of thine heart. Commit thy way unto the LORD; trust also in him; and he shall bring it to pass.*
Psalms 37:4-5

*IF thou ...shalt honour [the LORD], not doing thine own ways, nor finding thine own pleasure, nor speaking thine own words: Then shalt thou **delight** thyself in the LORD; and I will cause thee to ride upon the high places of the earth, and feed thee with the heritage of Jacob thy father: for the mouth of the LORD hath spoken it.*
Isaiah 58:13-14

Often people interpret the promise of Psalms 37:4 to mean that when they find delight in God, He is their magic genie waiting to give them anything they wish. But Isaiah turns that *delight* phrase into one of God's IF statements. He says, IF you honor the Lord; IF you do things His way; IF you do things to bring Him pleasure; IF you speak the words He wants you to say, then you will *delight* yourself in the Lord. In other words, as you honor the Lord with your lifestyle, find your pleasure in the path He sets your feet upon, and speak the words He wants you to speak, then you will know true delight and will be able to experience things you never dreamed of doing before. While it is important to set goals and dream dreams, don't get so locked into your own desires that you miss out on the exciting high places in life that God wants to give you, IF you do things His way.

Prayer: *Lord Jesus, I have a long list of things I desire to do and be and receive in my life, but help me to ask you first what you want me to do and be and have in my life. I want to find my delight in the path you choose for me so that my life can bring honor to you. Amen.*

Week 35 Review

Number from 1-15 the phrases from the five verses in this week's lessons. Number them in the same order that you studied them.

____ In all thy ways acknowledge him, and he shall direct thy paths.

____ and he shall bring it to pass.

____ of thine heart. Commit thy way unto the LORD; trust also in him;

____ If we confess our sins, he is faithful and just to forgive us our sins,

____ and lean not unto thine own understanding.

____ as some men count slackness; but is longsuffering to us-ward,

____ and to cleanse us from all unrighteousness.

____ but that all should come to repentance.

____ If ye keep my commandments, ye shall abide in my love;

____ and abide in his love.

____ The Lord is not slack concerning his promise,

____ Trust in the LORD with all thine heart;

____ not willing that any should perish,

____ Delight thyself also in the LORD: and he shall give thee the desires

____ even as I have kept my Father's commandments,

Memory Verse: 1 John 1:9 (Day 171); 2 Peter 3:9 (Day #172)

Additional Memory Verses: John 15:10 (Day #173); Proverbs 3:5-6 (Day #174); Psalms 37:4-5 (Day 175).

Week 36

Wrapping It All Up

For the past 35 weeks we have discussed a variety of topics ranging from knowing and obeying the Bible, heroes of the faith, salvation requirements, sins to get rid of, to fruits of righteousness to add to your faith. This week we will wrap up with lessons on the two roads that lead to Heaven or Hell. Your final destination will be determined by the choices you make during your life.

Day #176   Which Road Will You Choose?

He is in the way of life that keepeth instruction:
but he that refuseth reproof erreth.
Proverbs 10:17

Jesus talked about two roads to travel in life.[138] One road was very wide and fun to travel, and most people chose that easy road. The other road was narrow and not as inviting as the wide road. Not very many people chose that road. But the wide road led to death, and the narrow road led to life. Solomon said that those who follow instructions walk on the way to life while those who refuse correction will walk on the path that leads away from God. Which path will you choose?

Prayer: *Lord Jesus, help me to listen and obey the instructions from my parents and those who are older than me so that I too can walk the path of life that will lead me to Heaven after this life is over.*

Day #177   Wages Of Sin Or Gift Of God?

For the wages of sin is death; but the gift of God is
eternal life through Jesus Christ our Lord.
Romans 6:23

Jesus told a story of two men who lived near each other. One was very rich, had beautiful clothes, and the best food money could buy; but the other one, named Lazarus, was so poor that he had to beg for the crumbs that fell from the rich man's table. He was also sickly and had sores on his body. He didn't have medicine and bandages to take care of his sores, so stray dogs came and licked his sores. The rich man could easily have shared some of his food and given Lazarus some medicine and bandages for his sores, but he didn't. He was too selfish!

One day Lazarus died, and the angels carried him away to Heaven. The rich man was probably happy that the dirty beggar wasn't sitting at his gate anymore. But soon the rich man died also, and instead of angels carrying him to Heaven, he was taken to Hell. He could see Lazarus

---

[138] Matthew 7:13-14.

having a good time, and he begged Abraham to bring just a drop of water to cool his tongue because he was tormented in the flames of Hell. Abraham refused and told him he had his chance to make the right choices when he was alive, but he didn't. Now it was too late.[139]

Every boy and girl who is born into this world is born into sin. If the person does not become born again and obey all of God's Word while they are alive, Paul said they would receive death for their sins when they die, but those who are born again and faithfully obey God's Word will receive the gift of eternal life forever with Jesus. You only have one chance to live and make the right choice for your destination after your earthly life. Choose Jesus and the way of life.

Prayer: *Lord Jesus, help me to study your Word every day and make the right choices in my life so that when I die, I will receive the gift of eternal life with you forever and ever. Amen.*

Day #178   Is Your Name In The Book Of Life?

And I saw the dead, small and great, stand before God; and the books were opened: and another book was opened, which is the book of life: and the dead were judged out of those things which were written in the books, according to their works. And whosoever was not found written in the book of life was cast into the lake of fire.
Revelation 20:12, 15

He that overcometh shall inherit all things; and I will be his God, and he shall be my son. But the fearful, and unbelieving, and the abominable, and murderers, and whoremongers, and sorcerers, and idolaters, and all liars, shall have their part in the lake which burneth with fire and brimstone: which is the second death.
Revelation 21:7-8

There is nothing greater in this life than to know that you are God's son or daughter. Everyone is born into the family of sin, but Jesus has made the way for you to be born into His family. You can remain in the family of sin, or you can make the choice to be born again into the family of God.

---

[139] Luke 16:19-31

Everyone who chooses to be born into God's family will be rewarded, but those who are not born again will be judged and punished.[140]

Prayer: *Lord Jesus, nothing pleases me more than to be called a child of God. Help me to repent often and keep sin out of my life so that one day I will hear you say to me, "Well done, thou good and faithful servant...enter thou into the joy of the Lord."[141] Amen.*

Day #179   The Blessing Of Entering The City

Blessed are they that do his commandments, that they may have right to the tree of life, and may enter in through the gates into the city.
Revelation 22:14

Chapter 22 of Revelation gives a very vivid description of the holy city called Heaven. You may think you can imagine how beautiful it will be, but the Bible says that you have never heard or seen anything to compare with the beauty of that place.[142] John wrote in the above verse that those who obey God's commands are blessed and have the right to eat from the Tree of Life and go inside the gates of that city. You do not want to miss seeing and living in that city. Make sure you know the rules for receiving the right to enter the gates and live there forever.

Prayer: *Lord Jesus, when I read the description of that beautiful city you are preparing for your Church, I get so excited and eager to see it. I have never lived anywhere that beautiful in my whole life. I intend to do whatever I need to do to please you and live in that beautiful new home for eternity. Amen.*

Day #180   Fight The Good Fight Of Faith

For I am now ready to be offered, and the time of my departure is at hand. I have fought a good fight, I have finished my course, I have kept the faith: Henceforth there is laid up for me a crown of righteousness, which the Lord, the righteous judge, shall give me at that day: and not to me only,

---

[140] Psalms 96:10-13.
[141] Matthew 25:23.
[142] 1 Corinthians 2:9.

but unto all them also that love his appearing.
2 Timothy 4:6-8

When the Apostle Paul started on his Christian journey to Heaven, he had many enemies who did not want to see him live for Jesus. Many times he was beaten, jailed, robbed, shipwrecked, and even left for dead one time, but God raised him up again.[143] Sometimes people get the wrong idea that living for Jesus is a walk through a rose garden, and nothing bad will happen to them once they are God's child. Don't be confused. Good and bad things happen to everyone. You are born into this life as a sinner, and when you decide to follow Jesus, the devil gets mad; he continually tries every trick he can think of to make you change your mind and join his side again. When Paul wrote these verses to Timothy, he was awaiting execution for his faith, but he was not sad. He said that he had fought a good fight and had kept his faith through it all. He was looking forward to being rewarded with a crown of righteousness from the Lord.

As a child of God, you will have good times and bad times, but don't be discouraged. If you remain obedient and faithful through everything that happens in your life, God has a crown waiting for you in the next life. Be faithful!

Prayer: *Lord Jesus, sometimes people laugh at me for being a Christian, but I want to let my light shine brightly for you even if my friends don't like the way I live. Let me be a witness of your saving power so I can bring my friends to know you in the power of the born again experience. I am looking forward to the day you welcome me into the beautiful city you have prepared for everyone who obeyed your commands. Amen.*

---

[143] 2 Corinthians 11:23-33; Acts 14:19-20.

Week 36 Review

Find the following words in the grid below.

Book – Choose – Christ – City – Crown – Dogs – Eternal – Faithful – Fearful – Fight – Finish – Flames – Gates – Gift – Heaven – Jesus – Judge – Lazarus – Liars – Life – Money – Narrow – Revelation – Reward – Road – Sin – Travel – Tree – Wages – Wide.

H	R	C	I	T	Y	Z	M	O	H	B	F	O	Z	H	X
T	K	D	J	U	D	G	E	O	N	W	A	G	E	S	S
F	O	T	Z	S	P	C	R	E	N	J	Z	M	C	I	H
I	O	X	R	E	W	A	R	D	N	E	P	N	H	N	R
G	B	R	E	L	I	A	R	S	T	S	Y	I	R	I	O
J	R	A	T	E	I	D	G	K	R	U	L	N	I	F	A
S	U	C	E	V	R	F	N	Z	S	S	V	I	S	B	D
L	U	F	R	A	E	F	O	E	R	W	G	S	T	J	U
T	Y	J	N	R	F	A	I	Y	V	X	S	B	H	T	K
E	W	D	A	T	U	I	T	N	S	A	S	S	G	L	G
S	S	I	L	D	P	T	A	W	E	C	E	R	I	I	A
O	G	T	D	G	R	H	L	O	M	K	J	H	F	K	T
O	O	D	E	E	U	F	E	R	A	H	B	K	U	E	E
H	D	G	E	A	M	U	V	C	L	A	Z	A	R	U	S
C	E	T	E	F	I	L	E	W	F	W	I	E	O	T	C
G	U	U	U	N	A	R	R	O	W	L	J	I	S	Y	V

Memory Verse: Romans 6:23 (Day #177)

Additional Memory Verses: 2 Timothy 4:6-8 (Day #180)

Answers to Weekly Reviews

Week 1

1) T 2) F 3) T 4) F 5) F 6) F 7) F 8) F 9) T 10) T 11) T.

Week 2

<u>Across</u> – 2) Timothy 5) hope 6) answer 9) child 10) devil.
<u>Down</u> – 1) truth 3) memorize 4) bread 7) study 8) sin.

Week 3

1) 10 2) 9 3) 13 4) 12 5) 4 6) 11 7) 1 8) 2 9) 8 10) 3 11) 6 12) 7 13) 5.

Week 4

1) marriage 2) wife 3) husband 4) love 5) unbeliever 6) parents
7) children 8) home 9) submit 10) church 11) woman 12) man.

Week 5

right – promise – life – parents – rod – reproof – shame – Adonijah – king – obedience – 170 – respect – obey – unity.

Week 6

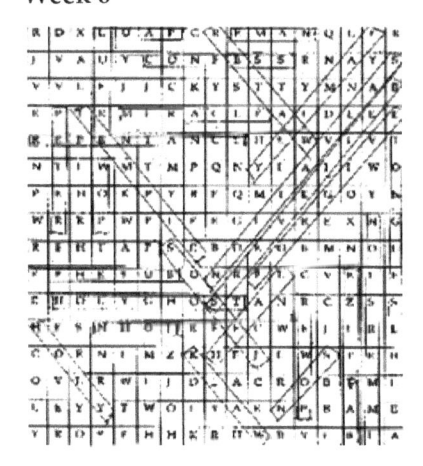

Week 7

Isaac – drink – camels – Esau – deceiver – Isaac – Rebekah – birthright – blessing – Leah – Rachel – Israel – 11 – Rachel – coat – Egypt – 30 – bowed – Amram – Jochebed – Red – tambourine – Nile – 3 – basket – Miriam – princess – 10.

Week 8

1) 7 2) 4 3) 1 4) 8 5) 2 6) 3 7) 6 8) 9 9) 5 10) 11 11) 10.

Week 9

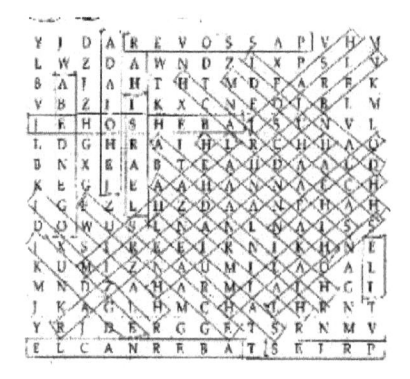

Week 10

1) F 2) F 3) T 4) F 5) F 6) T 7) T 8) F 9) T 10) T 11) T 12) F

Week 11

1) Moses 2) Mary 3) Amram 4) Esther 5) Jochebed 6) Solomon 7) Aquila
8) Aaron 9) Barnabas - 10) Mordecai 11) David 12) Priscilla 13) Miriam
14) Mark.

Week 12

Across: 5) praise 6) children 7) offend 8) name 9) righteousness 11) blessed. Down: 1) house 2) peacemakers 3) disciples 4) converted
10) greatest 12) last.

Week 13

1) 11 2) 5 3) 10 4) 2 5) 8 6) 1 7) 13 8) 7 9) 12 10) 3 11) 9 12) 6 13) 4.

Week 14

Israel – one – heart – soul – might – Lord – faith – baptism – God – Father – above – through – in – Word – was – made – flesh – beheld – grace – truth – Father – one – known – me – me – Father – in – in – myself – Father – in.

Week 15

1) Nicodemus 2) Jerusalem 3) Gospel 4) death 5) burial 6) resurrection
7) salvation 8) repentance 9) baptism 10) Holy Ghost 11) tongues
12) Cornelius.

Week 16

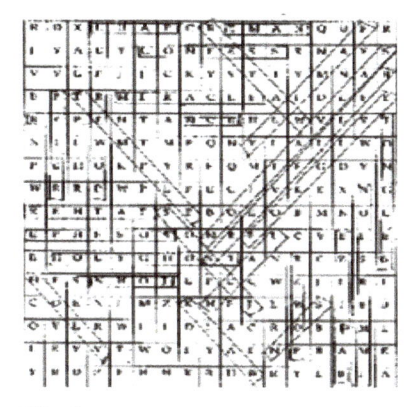

Week 17

1) F 2) F 3) T 4) F 5) F 6) T 7) T 8) F 9) T 10) T 11) T 12) F.

Week 18

<u>Across</u>: 4) bread 7) heaven 8) deliver 9) forgive 12) temptation 14) fire
<u>Down</u>: 1) healed 2) power 3) lied 5) thanksgiving 6) kingdom
10) confess 11) name 13) ears.

Week 19

Jeremiah – gods – pastors – knowledge – understanding – obey – report – behavior – pray – church truth – excited – house   clap – hands – sing – near – praise – listen – preaches.

Week 20

1) 8 2) 5 3) 11 4) 1 5) 12 6) 3 7) 10 8) 4 9) 6 10) 2 11) 7 12) 9.

Week 21

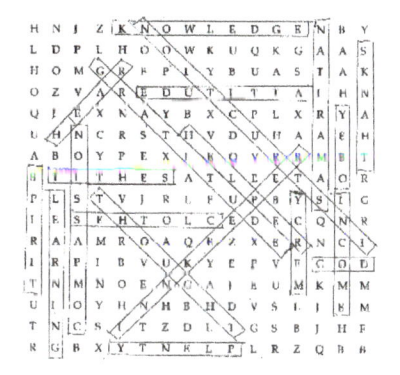

219

Week 22

1) goodness 2) peace 3) meekness 4) gentleness 5) love 6) temperance 7) joy 8) faith 9) longsuffering.

Week 23

1) F 2) T 3) F 4) T 5) F 6) T 7) T 8) F 9) T 10) T.

Week 24

<u>Across</u>: 3) wealth 4) unselfish 7) trespass 8) judge 11) forgive 12) mercy
<u>Down</u>: 1) share 2) blessing 5) sacrifice 6) apology 9) winner 10) repent.

Week 25

1 – 3 – 5 – 7 – 11 – 14 – 4 – 6 – 15 – 8 – 13 – 9 – 2 – 12 – 10.

Week 26

1) F 2) T 3) F 4) F 5) T 6) F 7) T 8) T 9) T 10) F 11) T 12) F.

Week 27

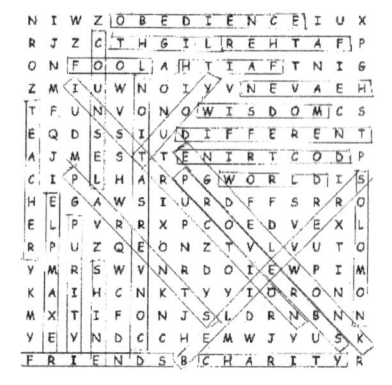

Week 28

1) 7 2) 9 3) 1 4) 11 5) 6 6) 10 7) 5 8) 3 9) 4 10) 2 11) 8 12) 12.

Week 29

1) Lying – Pride – Kicking the cat – Killing innocent people – Evil thoughts – Troublemaker in the family – Running around doing wrong things – Tell lies in court – Hate the policeman. 2) Saul 3) Those who are proud. 4) The humble in spirit. 5) Something shameful, strongly disliked or hated 6) Lying lips 7) Those who tell the truth 8) The wolf was coming to get the sheep. 9) Lying on purpose to persuade others to believe your lie.

Week 30

Across: 1) anger 2) vain 6) creator 8) praise 9) bragging 10) mind
11) trust. Down: 1) anxiety 3) fear 4) Demetrius 5) afraid 7) Diana.

Week 31

Across: 3) work 6) alone 9) gossip 11) talebearer 12) lazy 13) weep
Down: 1) anger 2) wood 4) rejoice 5) panic 7) strength 8) friendship
10) jealousy 13) wrath.

Week 32

Owner – body – sins – cross – attitude – glory – holy – Temple – mistreat – care – Exercise – healthy – activities – spirit – neglect – balance – sleep – rest – worrying – problem – health – laziness – work.

Week 33

1) 5 2) 12 3) 6 4) 9 5) 11 6) 2 7) 10 8) 4 9) 3 10) 7 11) 8 12) 1.

Week 34

1) F 2) T 3) T 4) T 5) F 6) F 7) F 8) T 9) T 10) T 11) F 12) T.

Week 35

12 – 15 – 14 – 1 – 11 – 4 – 2 – 6 – 7 – 9 – 3 – 10 – 5 – 13 – 8.

Week 36

Index

A

Aaron 61, 91, 178, 281
Abednego 79, 80
ability 44, 57, 85, 101, 109, 196, 203, 205
abomination 220, 222, 224
Abraham 57, 275
Adam 35, 116, 203
Adonijah 44, 280
Aesop 222
Ahab 146
Ahasuerus 92
Andrew 108, 111, 119
angel 106, 109, 111, 125, 260
angry 9, 44, 59, 76, 79, 84, 93, 150, 187, 228, 236, 237, 238,
Answer ... 18, 23, 87, 141, 182, 205, 262
Anxiety 228
Apollos 94
apologize 157, 237
Aquila and Priscilla 94
argue 156
Arguments 156
attitude 44, 45, 57, 60, 84, 85, 100, 107, 164, 197, 215, 221, 242, 245, 284
authority 36, 45, 46, 221
Azariah 78, 80

B

baptism 114, 122, 123, 128, 130, 131, 132, 281
Barnabas 94, 281
behavior 11, 15, 17, 44, 68, 85, 153, 172, 242, 282
believer 9, 106, 123, 130, 158, 208
Bible ... 3, 7, 9, 10, 11, 12, 16, 17, 21, 22, 23, 24, 27, 29, 30, 32, 38, 45, 50, 53, 61, 75, 78, 85, 86, 96, 106, 131, 134, 144, 157, 158, 160, 164, 173, 186, 188, 194, 195, 203, 209, 210, 215, 216, 228, 229, 235, 236, 243, 244, 245, 249, 261, 264, 268, 272, 276, 292, 294, 295
blessing 9, 57, 58, 99, 164, 186, 251, 256, 280, 283
blood 49, 116, 140, 215, 220
body 36, 51, 107, 115, 138, 141, 157, 203, 242, 243, 245, 261, 274, 284
Book Of Life 275
born again 106, 122, 132, 275, 277
bragging 15, 229, 284
brother .57, 58, 60, 61, 63, 91, 131, 156, 165, 188, 194, 215, 221, 235, 257, 259, 260

C

children . 7, 9, 10, 11, 23, 29, 35, 37, 38, 44, 45, 46, 49, 50, 51, 53, 61, 69, 76, 83, 91, 92, 99, 100, 101, 107, 108, 164, 166, 187, 188, 212, 216, 234, 245, 249, 256, 257, 260, 261, 262, 266, 267, 280, 281
choices 86, 145, 187, 209, 242, 272, 275
Christian ... 11, 17, 18, 29, 38, 49, 61, 84, 109, 110, 116, 158, 159, 174, 180, 196, 197, 208, 277, 292
Church 36, 61, 62, 94, 99, 108, 133, 151, 174, 179, 180, 267, 276
comfort 69, 86, 100, 133, 173
commandments 16, 29, 30, 32, 71, 106, 138, 139, 141, 220, 267, 270, 276
commitment 21
compassion 165, 250
Competition 100
complaining 107, 195, 196, 203, 249
Considerate 186
content 11, 70, 204
conversation ... 122, 208, 212, 214, 267
Cornelius 125, 126, 281
correction .. 17, 18, 44, 45, 46, 50, 53, 86, 274
Correction 44, 45, 50

counsel 209
cross ... 51, 106, 116, 140, 141, 242, 245, 284
Cursing 229

D

Daniel 15, 46, 78, 79, 80
Darius 78
Day of Pentecost 106, 120, 123
delight 27, 29, 32, 45, 173, 222, 224, 269, 270
determination 202, 205
devil 21, 49, 116, 277, 280
disciples 99, 100, 108, 115, 119, 122, 123, 124, 126, 130, 132, 139, 144, 172, 173, 179, 250, 267, 281
disobedience 194, 220
doctrine 17, 18, 210
dreams 59, 63, 85, 261, 269

E

Egypt 59, 60, 61, 63, 91, 220, 280
elders 156
Elisha 145, 249, 253
Elkanah 75
enemies 86, 140, 141, 202, 221, 277
Ephesus 94, 114, 130, 134, 174, 182, 204, 215, 228
Esau 58, 63, 280
Esther 32, 89, 92, 93, 281
Eutychus 251, 252, 253
Eve 35, 116
example 17, 36, 38, 51, 77, 94, 110, 172, 202, 208, 243, 264
Exercise 157, 243, 245, 284
experience . 11, 100, 116, 123, 130, 186, 267, 269, 277, 292
Ezra 32, 268

F

faith ... 11, 23, 60, 79, 100, 101, 109, 110, 111, 114, 124, 157, 158, 159, 160,
172, 179, 180, 182, 196, 208, 215, 249, 272, 276, 277, 281, 283
family ... 9, 11, 35, 36, 38, 57, 58, 59, 60, 63, 68, 75, 83, 91, 94, 96, 99, 107, 108, 122, 124, 132, 146, 151, 164, 203, 220, 224, 244, 248, 249, 251, 257, 258, 259, 275, 283
father ... 35, 43, 44, 46, 49, 50, 68, 71, 76, 77, 83, 87, 107, 156, 256, 269
fear .. 23, 44, 86, 209, 228, 230, 236, 259, 284
Fear 106, 230, 236, 260
fearful 93, 229, 230, 275
fears 173, 230
follow. 16, 35, 36, 37, 49, 59, 76, 77, 86, 87, 92, 107, 110, 116, 123, 150, 153, 180, 182, 208, 274, 277
fool 209
forgave .... *See* forgive
forgiveness 86, 100, 101, 131, 187, 189, 215, 266, 267
friends 49, 70, 78, 84, 95, 107, 140, 159, 164, 178, 186, 187, 210, 215, 217, 221, 234, 235, 236, 237, 244, 257, 258, 277
frightened 173, 229, 236
fruit .. 101, 172, 173, 174, 178, 179, 180, 182
Fruit of the Spirit 172
furious 236
furnace 30, 32, 79

G

Gabriel 106, 111
Garden of Eden 35, 116
Gehazi 145, 249, 253
gentle 156, 157, 178, 221
gentleness 172, 174, 178, 283
give 15, 23, 24, 29, 30, 44, 45, 46, 51, 57, 58, 63, 68, 69, 75, 101, 108, 124, 133, 139, 144, 145, 150, 151, 153, 156, 157, 164, 165, 166, 168, 173, 188, 194, 196, 204, 208, 214, 215, 216, 236, 244, 245, 269, 270, 276

God 9, 10, 11, 12, 15, 16, 17, 18, 21, 22, 23, 25, 27, 29, 30, 31, 32, 35, 36, 37, 38, 44, 45, 46, 50, 57, 58, 59, 60, 61, 63, 67, 68, 69, 71, 75, 76, 77, 78, 79, 83, 84, 85, 86, 87, 91, 92, 93, 95, 99, 101, 106, 107, 108, 109, 110, 112, 114, 115, 116, 118, 119, 122, 124, 125, 131, 132, 133, 138, 139, 141, 144, 145, 146, 150, 152, 153, 156, 158, 160, 164, 166, 168, 173, 175, 179, 182, 186, 187, 188, 194, 195, 196, 202, 203, 205, 208, 209, 212, 214, 215, 216, 217, 220, 221, 222, 224, 228, 229, 230, 236, 242, 243, 245, 248, 249, 251, 253, 256, 260, 261, 262, 264, 266, 267, 268, 269, 274, 275, 276, 277, 281

God's Word ..10, 12, 15, 16, 17, 18, 21, 23, 25, 27, 29, 30, 31, 32, 37, 45, 46, 67, 79, 132, 150, 153, 160, 187, 196, 275

Goliath 83, 85, 87, 215, 216, 217

Goodness 178

Gospel 94, 116, 122, 123, 124, 125, 126, 158, 160, 257, 281

Gossip 234

gratitude 164, 197

Great Commission 122, 123

guard 38, 70, 158, 197, 268

H

habits 243

Hananiah 78, 80

Hannah 75, 80

happy ... 45, 51, 53, 70, 92, 99, 101, 151, 166, 196, 203, 234, 235, 257, 274

Hate 172, 224, 283

hateful 9, 140, 141, 195

healthy 36, 51, 53, 203, 243, 245, 284

heart 21, 31, 32, 30, 51, 53, 61, 76, 78, 85, 86, 87, 100, 102, 106, 108, 114, 124, 132, 138, 146, 150, 152, 160, 173, 179, 195, 198, 208, 215, 220, 221, 250, 268, 269, 270, 281

Heaven 16, 58, 100, 122, 123, 150, 158, 211, 235, 272, 274, 276, 277, 278

Hell 272, 274

Herod 108, 111

Holiness 214, 217

holy 16, 17, 23, 67, 68, 71, 116, 133, 144, 159, 212, 214, 215, 216, 229, 242, 245, 266, 276, 284

Holy Ghost 10, 106, 123, 124, 125, 130, 131, 141, 208, 242, 281

honest 16, 69, 145, 172, 196, 198

Honour 43, 68, 156, 164

hope 23, 24, 205, 280

humility 174, 221, 229

Husband 36, 95

I

idolatry 77

Immanuel 116

infant baptism 131

instruction . 16, 17, 18, 49, 166, 209, 274

intimidated 210

Isaac 57, 58, 280

Israel .. 29, 44, 46, 49, 58, 63, 75, 76, 77, 79, 80, 83, 84, 85, 87, 91, 92, 114, 116, 145, 146, 150, 153, 195, 214, 215, 221, 224, 248, 266, 268, 280, 281

J

Jacob 58, 59, 63, 103, 111, 269

Jairus 246, 250, 253

James 3, 87, 101, 119, 126, 146, 194, 198, 221, 264

jealous 59, 69, 84, 216, 234

Jealousy 234

Jehoiada 76, 80

Jehosheba 76, 80

Jeremiah 39, 150, 153, 202

Jerusalem 76, 77, 94, 106, 107, 111, 122, 126, 266, 268, 281

Jesus 9, 10, 15, 16, 17, 21, 22, 23, 24, 29, 30, 31, 35, 36, 37, 38, 41, 43, 44, 45, 49, 50, 51, 52, 57, 58, 60, 61, 62, 67, 68, 69, 70, 75, 76, 77, 79, 83, 84, 85, 86, 91, 92, 93, 94, 95, 99, 100, 101,

102, 103, 106, 107, 108, 109, 110, 111, 114, 115, 116, 118, 119, 122, 123, 124, 125, 126, 128, 130, 131, 132, 133, 134, 138, 139, 140, 141, 144, 145, 146, 150, 151, 152, 156, 157, 158, 159, 164, 165, 166, 167, 172, 173, 174, 175, 178, 179, 180, 182, 186, 187, 188, 189, 194, 195, 196, 197, 202, 203, 204, 206, 208, 209, 210, 214, 215, 216, 220, 221, 222, 223, 228, 229, 230, 234, 235, 236, 237, 242, 243, 244, 248, 249, 250, 251, 252, 253, 256, 258, 259, 260, 261, 264, 266, 267, 269, 274, 275, 276, 277, 278
Jesus' name 84, 100, 106, 116, 123, 124, 125, 130, 133, 221
Joash 76, 80
John 15, 16, 18, 71, 92, 94, 96, 106, 108, 115, 116, 119, 122, 130, 131, 132, 133, 134, 136, 138, 139, 141, 173, 208, 216, 217, 220, 236, 256, 262, 266, 267, 270, 276
Jonathan 212, 215, 217
Joseph 59, 60, 63, 103, 106, 107, 111
Joshua 18, 29, 32
Josiah 73, 77, 80
joy .51, 92, 109, 150, 172, 173, 276, 283

K

kindness 57, 76, 102, 178, 180, 215
Kingdom 29, 37, 91, 92, 95, 99, 100, 101, 122, 144, 179, 182

L

Laban 58
law 7, 9, 11, 16, 29, 31, 32, 49, 60, 63, 79, 114, 138, 172, 194, 198, 221, 259, 260, 292
Lazarus 274, 278
Laziness 235
lazy 202, 235, 284
Leah 58, 280
lie 16, 59, 69, 86, 138, 222, 224, 244, 256, 283

life 10, 11, 15, 16, 17, 21, 23, 29, 31, 36, 37, 38, 43, 49, 51, 59, 60, 61, 68, 75, 76, 77, 79, 84, 85, 86, 87, 91, 92, 93, 94, 95, 100, 106, 110, 115, 116, 123, 124, 132, 138, 150, 158, 159, 164, 167, 172, 173, 174, 180, 203, 204, 208, 209, 214, 221, 243, 245, 248, 249, 252, 256, 257, 261, 266, 267, 268, 269, 272, 274, 275, 276, 277, 280
light 17, 37, 51, 208, 209, 214, 242, 243, 277
listen 21, 49, 75, 84, 146, 153, 156, 158, 166, 167, 209, 221, 274, 282
longsuffering..... 172, 174, 266, 270, 283
love one another 139, 256
lying lips 222

M

Manasseh 266
Mark ..15, 31, 63, 94, 99, 100, 119, 122, 123, 124, 126, 173, 251, 281
Marriage 35, 69
Mary 94, 106, 107, 108, 111, 281
meditation 29, 195, 198
meekness 23, 156, 174, 178, 180, 182, 283
Memorize 21
Memory verse.. 18, 224, 231, 238, 245, 253, 262
Merciful 187
Meshach 79, 80
miracle 79, 106, 109, 111, 133, 248, 250, 251, 252, 253
Miriam 60, 61, 63, 91, 280, 281
Mishael 78, 80
Money 30, 32, 164, 278
Mordecai 89, 92, 93, 281
Moses. 29, 38, 51, 53, 60, 61, 63, 67, 71, 91, 114, 138, 214, 281
mother... 9, 35, 43, 44, 46, 49, 58, 59, 60, 63, 68, 71, 75, 76, 91, 94, 106, 107, 109, 110, 111, 178, 203, 235, 248, 249, 250, 253, 256

mouth 12, 21, 70, 83, 195, 198, 229, 230, 248, 269
music 83, 85, 87, 152, 164, 166, 292

N

Naaman 145, 195
Nain 250, 253
Nebuchadnezzar 15, 78, 79, 80, 268
New Birth 11, 122
Nicodemus 122, 126, 281

O

Obedience 16, 43, 46, 51, 139, 211
obey ... 16, 29, 30, 43, 44, 45, 46, 49, 51, 78, 79, 85, 93, 106, 107, 116, 123, 124, 138, 139, 141, 150, 153, 166, 173, 179, 182, 194, 208, 214, 220, 235, 267, 274, 275, 276, 280, 282
offend 31, 101, 281
offering 165
one God 57, 60

P

Panic 236
parents... 7, 9, 11, 37, 39, 43, 44, 45, 46, 49, 50, 51, 52, 53, 57, 59, 60, 63, 68, 69, 70, 75, 78, 92, 93, 107, 109, 110, 179, 186, 209, 221, 236, 243, 249, 250, 259, 261, 274, 280
Passover 77, 80, 107, 108, 111
pastor 37, 38, 150, 151, 153, 248, 249
patient 156, 205
pattern 35, 36, 37, 125, 130
Paul .. 23, 30, 69, 94, 109, 110, 111, 114, 123, 130, 133, 134, 150, 151, 154, 156, 157, 158, 159, 160, 174, 179, 180, 182, 204, 205, 208, 210, 215, 228, 234, 242, 243, 251, 253, 275, 277
peace 31, 43, 99, 101, 102, 109, 144, 172, 173, 174, 175, 214, 283
Pharaoh 59, 60, 63, 91
Philip 115, 116, 119

polite 68, 156
Potiphar 59
power ... 15, 58, 109, 114, 122, 133, 144, 195, 228, 229, 277, 282
praise 15, 61, 62, 91, 101, 151, 152, 153, 164, 179, 182, 196, 197, 198, 229, 230, 281, 282, 284
pray 11, 31, 57, 69, 75, 78, 133, 140, 141, 144, 146, 150, 153, 158, 173, 195, 234, 243, 248, 256, 282
prayer 12, 29, 30, 58, 75, 93, 94, 108, 109, 140, 144, 146, 157, 158, 160, 173, 205, 229, 236, 249, 261, 266, 268
pride 220, 221
promise 15, 43, 68, 75, 114, 122, 132, 229, 236, 243, 260, 266, 268, 269, 270, 280
proud .... *See* pride
punishment 44, 141, 242, 266
pure 30, 31, 106, 109, 196, 198, 208
purity 30, 31, 156, 208

Q

quarrel 228

R

Rachel 58, 59, 280
Rebekah 57, 58, 63, 280
Redeemer 116
Rehoboam 49, 53
repent 31, 58, 85, 86, 123, 124, 131, 160, 188, 195, 266, 276, 283
repentance .85, 122, 124, 126, 130, 156, 266, 270, 281
represent 11, 186, 242
respect . 15, 43, 44, 45, 51, 67, 68, 69, 93, 100, 101, 156, 160, 209, 229, 280
reward 195, 196, 198, 214
Rhoda 108, 109, 111
Richard Wurmbrand 196
righteousness .. 17, 37, 86, 101, 179, 180, 236, 272, 276, 277, 281
role-model 110

royal law 194
rules 11, 29, 43, 44, 45, 46, 107, 124, 139, 140, 141, 220, 276
rumors 234

S

salvation 23, 116, 124, 125, 126, 130, 134, 159, 160, 272, 281
Samuel . 25, 75, 80, 83, 84, 87, 215, 216, 220, 221
Saul 83, 84, 85, 87, 94, 146, 216, 220, 221, 236, 283
saved 23, 92, 93, 123, 124, 125, 134, 138, 159, 210, 256, 260, 262
scripture ... 3, 9, 17, 21, 38, 43, 101, 107, 115, 122, 131, 172, 194, 198
Selfishness 187
servant 30, 57, 75, 83, 99, 111, 145, 156, 195, 249, 253, 276
Shadrach 79, 80
Shared 108
sharing .... *See* share
Shepherd 83, 87, 131
Shunem 249
sin 11, 16, 17, 21, 31, 60, 68, 116, 124, 131, 132, 145, 194, 198, 208, 214, 220, 237, 238, 266, 274, 275, 276, 280
Sing 61, 152
singing 23, 61, 63, 85, 87, 152, 153, 164, 182
sinner 116, 131, 215, 277
sister. 43, 60, 61, 91, 131, 156, 165, 194, 221, 256, 257, 260, 262
sleep ... 35, 142, 164, 179, 230, 243, 244, 245, 251, 284
Solomon .. 16, 39, 44, 45, 49, 51, 53, 92, 166, 196, 202, 209, 211, 234, 235, 257, 274, 281
Spirit 106, 115, 122, 124, 138, 141, 166, 168, 172, 174, 175, 180, 208, 242, 253
steal ... 16, 21, 68, 71, 114, 138, 204, 235
storm 173, 228, 259

strong . 29, 37, 51, 60, 93, 101, 114, 150, 151, 156, 157, 159, 160, 202, 203, 205, 215, 220, 222, 261
study 7, 11, 21, 22, 23, 24, 29, 30, 31, 36, 38, 45, 107, 115, 139, 150, 152, 157, 158, 173, 228, 243, 245, 275, 280
submit 36, 39, 150, 280

T

Tabernacle 75, 80, 85, 87, 91
talebearer 234, 284
tattletales 234
temple 77, 92, 242
Temptation 49
tempted 21, 22, 49, 222, 228
Ten Commandments 29, 43, 61, 67, 79, 138, 194
tenderhearted 215
thankful 9, 23, 37, 67, 70, 75, 86, 114, 125, 130, 131, 151, 153, 158, 188, 243, 244, 248, 259, 266
thanks 108, 133, 144, 164
thanksgiving 144, 153, 282
thoughts ... 7, 30, 69, 195, 197, 224, 283
Time 151, 165
Timothy ... 17, 22, 23, 25, 29, 30, 49, 69, 70, 80, 87, 94, 109, 110, 111, 154, 156, 157, 158, 159, 160, 180, 208, 210, 211, 228, 231, 243, 277, 278, 280
tithe 164
tongues 125, 126, 130, 172, 281
trouble ... 16, 50, 60, 101, 138, 157, 220, 221, 222, 257, 260
true 15, 16, 18, 70, 76, 77, 78, 79, 85, 114, 116, 150, 196, 198, 208, 223, 235, 258, 266, 269
trust 45, 77, 79, 101, 150, 158, 173, 209, 230, 243, 250, 259, 268, 269, 270, 284
truth 15, 16, 18, 22, 92, 115, 132, 150, 153, 156, 160, 216, 222, 223, 248, 280, 281, 282, 283
two roads 272, 274

U

Unbeliever 37
Unity 45
unselfish 36, 57, 164, 186, 283

W

wife .. 35, 36, 39, 57, 59, 63, 85, 95, 145, 195, 257, 261, 280
wisdom 16, 18, 44, 46, 51, 59, 78, 92, 107, 203, 209
words. 12, 16, 17, 18, 22, 30, 32, 38, 39, 49, 53, 61, 68, 70, 71, 80, 100, 101, 111, 115, 119, 125, 126, 131, 134, 139, 153, 157, 158, 160, 168, 172, 174, 194, 195, 198, 202, 209, 211, 216, 217, 223, 224, 229, 230, 234, 236, 237, 253, 269, 278
work 11, 37, 44, 51, 57, 60, 69, 91, 95, 139, 141, 165, 172, 179, 202, 203, 204, 205, 209, 210, 235, 243, 244, 245, 257, 261, 284
worker 202, 203
worry 144, 243
worship ... 67, 68, 71, 75, 76, 77, 79, 85, 87, 92, 101, 114, 151, 152, 166, 214, 228
wrong 16, 17, 21, 22, 45, 49, 50, 76, 85, 86, 124, 132, 145, 146, 151, 156, 157, 187, 188, 189, 220, 222, 224, 266, 277, 283

Y

youth 23, 208

Z

Zarephath 248, 253
Zedekiah 268

About the Author

Pam with her Grandkids

Pam Eddings has more than twenty years of experience in writing, editing, and proofreading Christian literature, and has assisted in the making of dozens of books and hundreds of articles by both Apostolic and secular writers.

She draws from a lifetime of teaching Sunday School classes, and speaking at seminars, retreats and special events. As a licensed minister and prison Chaplain, she has taught weekly Bible studies for more than thirteen years to thousands of men and women inmates.

Pam is also a skilled singer, musician, and music instructor, and plays active musical and teaching roles in her local church. She has three sons, three daughters-in-law, two grandsons and three granddaughters. Her home is in Springfield, Missouri.

Order ONE-YEAR BIBLE QUIZ
373 pages
at eddingspam@gmail.com

One-Year Bible Quiz

1189 Q&As for Teaching
Genesis to Revelation

PAM EDDINGS

Order BIBLE GEMS TO START YOUR DAY
at edddingspam@gmail.com

BIBLE Gems
TO START YOUR DAY

PAM EDDINGS

Pam's writing is designed for those who hunger for righteousness and a closer walk with God.
Rev. Carroll Bushnell

Pam's wisdom comes from the many challenges that life has thrown at her. Your heart and mind will be blessed and enriched.
Rev. Glenn Murphy

Her musings and writings have been a source of inspiration to so many over the years.
Lynda Allison Doty, PhD

Thought-Provoking, Inspirational and Helpful Bible Lessons for Each Morning of the Year.
By Pam Eddings

Bible Gems
To Start Your Day

Pam Eddings

Order RIGHT STEPS FOR KIDS
at edddingspam@gmail.com

To Order Additional Copies of Pam's books:

ONE YEAR BIBLE QUIZ

BIBLE GEMS

Or

RIGHT STEPS FOR KIDS

Please EMAIL her at:

eddingspam@gmail.com